Polenta at Midnight

DEAR CAROLINE & PHIL

THIS IS A SMALL PIECE OF
PHIL'S HERITAGE
IT IS THE STORY OF TWO
WONDERFUL CULTURES
JOINING TOGETHER, SHARED
IN CELEBRATION OF YOUR
WEDDING DAY!
SEPTEMBER 8TH 2012

Polenta at Midnight

Tales of Gusto and Enchantment
in North York

Glenn Carley

Véhicule Press

Published with the generous assistance of The Canada Council for the Arts, and the Book Publishing Industry Development Program of the Department of Canadian Heritage (BPIDP).

Cover design: David Drummond
Set in Minion and Caslon by Simon Bodoni
Printed by Marquis Printing Inc.

LIBRARY AND ARCHIVES CANADA CATALOGUING IN PUBLICATION

Carley, Glenn
Polenta at midnight : tales of gusto and enchantment
in North York / Glenn Carley

ISBN 1-55065-224-9

1. Carley, Glenn—Family. 2. Italian Canadians—Ontario—
Toronto—Biography.
3. Italian Canadians—Ontario—Toronto—Social life and customs.
4. North York (Toronto, Ont.)—Biography. I. Title.

FC3099.N69Z49 2007   971.3'541   C2007-900592-6

Published by Véhicule Press, Montréal, Québec, Canada
www.vehiculepress.com

Distribution in Canada: LitDistCo
orders@litdistco.ca

Printed and bound in Canada on 100% post-consumer recycled paper.

Per Lina

Love is the life of man.

–Emanuel Swedenborg, 1763.

Signore e Signori, Ladies and Gentlemen

An address to the audience of the Living Opera

∿

Come with me to *Garibaldi's* Court and I will tell you tales of
gusto and enchantment.
We will sing, dance, laugh, cry and eat polenta at midnight, al fresco.
I promise you homemade red wine and frittata.
Have some more! For me!
We will work hard, and then we will rest.
Always there will be the *lezione*: something to learn and then
something to eat.
Together we will sing in the living opera and, like *Il Vagabondo*
You will make a life too.

Contents

Act I

Scene 1.

A Sauce-Making Tableau. *Canto* in Red

The English guy spends the day making sauce with the Italian guy

"The tomatoes are ready? No, I don't believe it! It is not possible."
For months I send reminders to Angelo and to his landlady Luisa that I must make *la bella salsa*, the beautiful tomato sauce this year. In fact, I must make everything this year. I am captivated—no, enchanted by the state of gusto! It is—how do you say it—the gateway to paradise. I am the student and it is *Salsa la Scuola* that I must attend.

My enthusiastic response holds their attention. They pause. Could it be that he really is interested in the old ways? Later, they will gaze at me curiously with smiles on their faces. It is a drama: red-as-fire. The tomatoes are early not because we got too much rain in July but because we got too much hot weather in June. It is too much. The alarm is sounded. I cannot be away when they make it this time. I must drop everything or I am doomed to be the ill-fated student.

Several years earlier, (*shrug shoulders here*) I made my wish known to my mother-in-law, Lina, and to Angelo:

"You have to let me make the sauce with you this year," I plead desperately, "and I don't mean *help* to make the sauce. No, you must teach me the way. Share your heritage. Think of it as working through me to teach the kids. They are half-Italian and they must learn about this side of themselves. Do you want them to lose the old ways?" I say raising my eyes and my shoulders in a dialect-act of clear blackmail.

I see a flicker of something in Lina's eyes but the old guy looks like he has not heard me.

"Ahh, Lina, you *comprendi! Grazie,*" I say in my best Italian.

I am relentless at dinner, after dinner or over *espresso* during cool evenings on lawn chairs in front of the garage. It pays off. Suddenly, I am given two days' notice. It is September.

"We are making it on *giovedi.* You must come early," Lina says without fanfare.

"I am not retired. I have to go into work," I complain to Mary, my—how do they say it—*mia moglie,* in the evening.

"What can I tell you? When they are ready, you have to go," she says.

I complete my meeting and leave work early to speed east across the 401, fifth gear from Mississauga to North York, fourth gear to Jane and Sheppard; finally, first gear and park at 23 Rita Drive. My work clothes are in the trunk. It is twelve minutes after eleven and I drop the checkered flag. I know that I am too late the moment I pull into the driveway and see the hose out, the assortment of steel pots and plastic colanders set on their edges to dry and Angelo beginning to squeegee the clean wet concrete in front of the garage.

"Dammit!" I say in my worst English. I am frustrated. I explain that I came as fast as I could. "You think I am an English tourist, still, after all these years," I snarl in defeat.

I feel like weeping. Lina sees it in my eyes. Angelo is already in his own masculine world, taking apart the silver tomato machine. He moves on to the next task in the sequence with little to no thought about what his *Inglese* just missed.

"You have to do the sauce when the tomatoes are ready" (*cock your head to the left, open up your hands at the waist, tilt your face up and bring your mouth corners down*), is all I can salvage from this tragic scene.

Later that month, in the gentle way of women, Lina concedes and picks up a bushel of tomatoes for me from the little variety store across the road. She sends my wife north with the clean purple twenty-litre pails we call *vin bon* containers, the plastic colanders, some pots and a hand grinder. But this is not the real way. It is the hobby-way, tourist class.

Time passes. Death comes and goes. I convince myself to give up. I will always be a tourist. I cannot speak the language and there is a mysterious psychology that keeps these people from understanding my need to learn, my need to love them. They are not teachers, they are doers. If you are lucky enough to be around or, better still, to live there, you may partake, otherwise forget it.

Seasons pass.

Suddenly there is hope. Like an omen, I am told to be present on a Thursday. It is the day the tomatoes are ready and we have time to do it. It is now late August.

"When do you want me there?" I ask.

"You come in the morning," is the reply. Very polite, with an intonation suggesting that I am a guest, I don't need to get up early and after all I have such a long way to travel from Bolton...

"No, really," I persist, "what time do you start?"

"You should be here by 7:30," comes a more definitive reply.

"Okay, *perfetto*! I am there by 7 a.m.," I announce with resolve.

I arrive at exactly 7. It has been an exquisite drive down Hwy 400 with a coffee and a toasted buttered bagel. John Coltrane plays "Live at the Village Vanguard" triumphantly on the car stereo.

"I am going live," I laugh to myself, my sense of free-jazz adventure intact.

I pull into the new golden driveway of North York. Luisa is in the garage. There are two big, plastic, water-filled tubs with bright tomatoes bobbing on fire. At the back, by the workbench, newspaper is spread out and more tomato-flames languish on top.

"Ahh, you are here," Luisa says, in the clipped accent of a woman who has learned the English language well, but prefers the fluidity of her mother tongue. "You are early! Good!"

Angelo is in the back setting up the tomato machine. He hears the noise and ambles forward to say: "Oh-oh, *Il Vagabondo* is here!"

"It is I," I say with a flourish.

"You are on time," he says.

"Do you think I am a tourist? I have come to work, not to talk," I say in the same dramatic, clipped cadence of an *Inglese* parrot who dropped out of Italian night school once, but later flew back in redemption.

I must tell you that I cannot speak *Italiano* beyond pigeon phrases, so when I feel like it, I step out of the fluidity of my mother tongue to be *the burlone*, the jester.

Quickly, for it is their way, I am put to work by Luisa. My first job is to wash the remaining dirt from bobbing tomatoes. I place the clean ones into a new bushel basket. It has an old perforated hockey jersey draped into it, forming a natural second sieve. You want to get as much water off as you can. We place the damaged tomatoes aside and later we will cut off the tops and all of the black marks. The debris will be placed into a separate metal salad bowl for depositing into the compost at the back.

"How do you know which tomatoes are good to buy?" I ask.

"Ahh," she says wistfully. "A tomato is a tomato, they are all good, you just know!"

It is my first authentic, south-central Italian lesson of the morning. *La prima lezione!* They come in the morning or in the evening or in the middle of the day. You must watch for them!

"This is how I will buy the tomatoes next year," I say to her. If my English friends or the children ask, this is what I will tell them.

The bushels are ready.

"No, you do not carry them to the back," Luisa cries out. "I have just the thing!" She goes to the side of the house and pulls out a custom-built cart to transport the bushels to the backyard. It is another lesson in *Garibaldi's* Court, pure and simple. Never do yourself what the machine can do for you.

"*Macchina* (ma-key-na)," I say over and over.

Angelo is there, at the back, putting the final touches on the tomato machine. He fits the metal sieve on the end and tells me how it broke last year. Luisa sits us down in front of another bushel basket and a huge metal salad bowl. I am instructed how to cut the tomatoes. Cut the fatter round ones into fours. Cut the long thin ones in half. My mother-in-law used to tell me to cut the long thin ones down the centre, lengthwise and now I know why. If you do it that way then you divide the harder core in two: the pieces are smaller and won't break the sieve. Luisa keeps the cores in, but you can cut the cores out. Angelo prefers the cores out but (*he shrugs his shoulders*) that is the way she makes it.

Everyone makes it their own way, it depends what you like—this is the third, beautiful *Mezzogiorno* lesson.

I am happy in sauce school. I am not going to drop out. I am in the presence of ancient ways with two elders who let me be around. We are enjoying the day and the company, while yellow jackets sip clear drippings of cut tomatoes. The sun has not yet come around to the back. You can tell it is going to get hot but, for now, we are cool. I see the squat, rusty burner over by the yard barn, the propane tank and the huge silver pot that the tomato jars go into. I pop a fresh piece of tomato into my mouth and pretend I can feel the spirit of it. It whisks me back to times in Italy. *Auguri.* Like a lucky ethereal wanderer, I am witness to a thousand stories. I listen to the tales and learn to speak them. I taste them now, on the roof of my mouth. They cling to me like the strong smell of *basilica* from the sprig hooked on the umbrella post at the patio table. I am in the shade. A breeze takes me fully into each moment where I "consider the lilies"—there is no rush—and I know exactly what is happening to me and why. It is the enchantment of *The Court of Garibaldi.* It is—how do you say it?—everything.

We continue slicing. After a time, Angelo accidentally drops a tomato on the ground. I say to Luisa that I have to start throwing the tomatoes on the ground to get the technique right.

"Write it down in your recipe book," she teases. "You are such a joker."

Angelo rises to prepare the sauce machine and I finish off the last bushel of tomatoes. Luisa gives me a *dimostrazione* on how to salvage the bruised and nasty ones (*malvagio*) we set aside. Rhythmically all the debris goes over again to the compost, next to the garden. Everything is in the compost. It is a work of art. I have seen these heaps beside gardens or dug underneath makeshift greenhouses. I marvel at the fact that on this 120-by-40 foot lot there are systems everywhere. The garden is a study in engineering. Down the little alley between the hedge and the beans is where the grass clippings are dumped. I joke that Angelo plays *bocci* back here, out of sight when he is supposed to be working. The *fagiolini* form a high, narrow arch growing amidst the metal rebar fused together with wire. It is not an Italian garden unless there is rebar holding things up. You get it from someone you know.

I joke that Angelo goes into the cool recess between the beans and sleeps here when he is tired of working. The grass clippings are laid down in rows, holding in the moisture, scribbling the beautiful shade. To wander in among the beans, to feel them rub against you, the coolness, the robust smell, the whine of bugs is to immigrate to the enchanted place. The basil is laid out nicely. The tomato plants are gigantic. Always, they are taller than mine and I say to myself I should water them every day, but I never make the time to do it. The zucchini play hide and seek between turgid starry leaves but they are given away by their yellow flower heads most of the time. Home free! I love the way everything plays together. A drama: it is the height of order and organization, melody and libretto: *la musica*!

I walk back to see what Angelo is doing to the tomato machine. Luisa appears with a banana for each of us. We take a short break. Luisa tells us it is important to eat the *frutta* and then she disappears back into the house.

Angelo and I finish our bananas and prepare to crush the tomatoes. The machine is ready. I carry a huge metal salad bowl filled with tomato slices over to the table onto which the contraption is bolted. We place a purple *vin bon* pail under the trough where the sauce will flow out. My job is to put the tomato slices into the reservoir on the top. Angelo will use the plastic plunger to guide them into the machine.

"So," I say, pausing for effect. "You see that I have the most *importante* job. The one you must go to the school for, for the Instruction."

Garibaldi raises his eyebrows, nods and smiles.

My comment reminds him of another time and another tale when we were discussing the difference between the Education and the Instruction. Angelo, like many in his Hometown, only went to grade five. This is as far as his Instruction went. Naturally, his Education is boundless, a product of the experience, trial and error, watching, patience, the cycles of the harvest. He knows I am teasing him about school and this is why he calls me the brigand, the wanderer: *Il Vagabondo.*

A small plastic bowl is placed at the end of the metal cone sieve to catch the tomato skins and core pieces that aren't pressed thru the holes. We will do a second pressing of these, afterwards.

"If you put it through a third time you will break the little cone like I did last year," he says with a boyish grin.

He is always experimenting. He learned a *lezione* on Luisa's tomato machine that she will not let him forget.

With a flip of the switch the motor is running. Thick red fluid begins to ooze down the little canal and into the twenty-litre pail. Everything is in slow motion now.

Luisa comes outside, as if on cue, to give me another sauce lesson. If you drape a tea towel over the edge of the pail and pull it forward to just about where the sauce falls in, it won't spatter on you or the patio. I take note, literally, in my little procedural book brought for this express purpose of capturing the practiced wisdom and sequence of the activity. I come from the world of the Instruction and I see *Garibaldi* and Luisa are both amused and pleased that I am being attentive to the process.

"I know you kept notes too, back in your Hometown!" I say, definitively.

Yellow jackets arrive to share the production.

"Why is it," I say to *Garibaldi*, "that every time I make something with you, wasps show up and I get stung? Do you do this on purpose?"

Once, in the early days of the Court, at the old house on lovely Rita, *Garibaldi*, my brother-in-law, and I go to Valencia and Ferlizzi's to look at the grapes, the *uva per vino*. We pick up thirty cases and put them in his van. I ride in the back with the wasps while he and Carmine ride in the cab. They do not believe I am stung once per case.

He remembers the joke well and laughs.

It is hotter now and the sun peeks around the corner at the back of the house. Ready or not. By 10:30 we complete the crushing. There are three pails of sauce. We are covered in spatters and I am very *contento*. In fact, you could say I am *molto contento*. Before we rest, we take the bowl of skins and cores and run them through the tomato machine one last time to salvage everything. Some sauce makers don't do it this way. Perhaps it will make the sauce sour like *mosto* pressed and added to new wine. Angelo takes a moment to demonstrate specifically how the cores broke the sieve. In between, there is another lesson. If you aren't quick you will miss it but I am smarter than I look.

"Nothing is wasted," I say quietly to myself to make the lesson permanent.

Luisa comes outside now, with a bottle of wine and two glasses. She is familiar enough with me now to know that I use the Mio glass with the green barber shop stripes on it and the white label. It is always my *bicchiere*. Everyone knows this. I feel a sense of exhilaration that I am working hard at 10:30 in the morning and drinking wine as if it were a coffee, as if I am bending the rules.

"Because you have worked you can drink wine now," Luisa says in her clipped accent.

The wine is full and warm and primitive and I cannot drink store-bought spirits anymore. I feel a subtle yet pervasive feeling of masculinity. I sense a similar presence of femininity throughout the entire passion play. How do I explain these feelings of enchantment to you? I think they are somehow linked to the order of the garden, the rows, the systems, the tendings to, the division of tasks from the soil to the table and back again. The cycle of seasons, the efficient current of life, the immensity and choreography of souls. Perceptions so slightly out of view that you have to be *Il Vagabondo* to see them. The Education, not the Instruction. It is a sacred moment as if I am at the burning bush and I must take off my sandals, be bathed in light, and do nothing other than listen, watch, and be humble. It is not that far from looking up at the morning sky, trying to gauge what the weather is going to be like and being right...time, patience, solitude and awareness—listening, letting things be and not trying to explain it all. You just know. It is like faith and tomatoes.

"I am a rich man," *Garibaldi* declares one day. "Not in terms of the money, but in terms of my life, *mia famiglia*."

And I am an apprentice in the dialect of his Court.

We finish the wine.

No one says it is time to go back to work. The resting time passes naturally. It is work time now and the primary thing is to complete this task and get to the next part of the sequence. I see Luisa over by the yard barn, rinsing one of the pots in the plastic fifty-gallon rain barrel. I gather up the knives, the salad bowls, the various tubs, the tomato-scooping-pots, the sieves and the strainers and I carry them all over to the water drum. Luisa leaves me to rinse. She goes back into the house to get the the salt and lids for the jars.

I stand in the shade and admire the jerry-built eavestrough on the side of the yard barn. It drains into the water barrel. It looks like the slender aluminium frame of a sliding glass door, riveted at a perfect angle onto the siding. I see a hose that leads from inside the house, along the side of the fence and out to the barrel. It transfers the condensation from the air conditioner. Nothing is wasted. Angelo takes me down into the basement to show me the system. Eureka! A small marvel in engineering. Luisa's husband Frank set it up. This hose leads from the air conditioner directly into the utility sink which fills up. A plastic tube in the drain will keep it from overflowing onto the floor. When the sink is full, go over to the wall and turn this valve here. Somehow the water then drains from the sink, along the hose and out into the water barrel. Luisa smiles as Angelo describes it. He is triumphant because at first he can't figure out how it works but he "studies" it and finally, he gets it.

"No matter—how do you say it?—what tragedy happens, we are self-sufficient," Luisa says, proudly.

She is right. There is magnificence to that. I continue to wash the equipment and set everything out in the sun to dry. Angelo comes over and gives me the what-for, for rinsing things directly in the barrel.

"That is not the way to do it," he says.

"I do it the way I am taught," I tell him.

"Then you have been taught wrong," he says logically.

By now, he has dismantled the tomato machine and I am washing the pieces. Luisa uses a small whisk broom with sharp, deliberate strokes to clean off the sieve. Soak the sieve first and then it will go better. I make a note to get a whisk broom.

The water cools my hands and arms. I enjoy the impromptu bath. There is a mystique to the Italian fifty-gallon barrel. When *Garibaldi* moved to El Dorado, he gave most of them away. I have a black one. Mine isn't doing anything right now. It is outside by the yard barn, overturned so mosquito larvae won't form in it and we don't all die horribly from West Nile virus. This is what happens if you have a barrel and don't use it properly. It is home to spiders and maple keys and leaf debris, empty, devoid of life, disconnected from its system, like old men. I remember six of them on Rita Drive. They stand at attention in a row on cement blocks along the wall of the garage at wine-making time. I ask where he gets them and Angelo says you just get them. You find them from people you know or from the guys at work or from someone your neighbour knows. It is like rebar, they are so useful. Some of the barrels had lard in them or vegetable oil and when they are all clean-looking inside, they need only to be rinsed with hose water. Now they are ready each fall, filled two inches from the brim with *muscato e carrignane e alicante* and covered with thick polyethylene plastic. You will hear the warm sizzle of fermenting wine in the afternoon. It is like bees whispering.

Luisa calls me over to the patio table and it too is covered with thick polyethylene plastic to keep the spatters from staining. It makes it so easy to clean. She shows me the lids, the wooden box of salt. She takes a sprig of *basilica* from the bunch hanging on the umbrella. It is now time to fill the jars. *Lezione cinque* or *sei*, I've lost count. First, take a teaspoon of salt and put it into the one-litre Mason jar. Next, take a sprig of basil and toss it into the jar as well. Now, fill the little pot that is field tested to hold exactly one-litre of sauce and pour the sauce into a cup-shaped funnel that fits into the neck of the Mason jar.

"Where am I going to get a cup-shaped funnel that fits the jars exactly?" I wonder to myself. "Mary will know," I say, nodding my head absentmindedly.

This is not a true lesson because perhaps women everywhere, in every country, know where everything is. It does not occur just in *Garibaldi's* Court.

"We already have one," Mary will tell me dryly, later, when I ask.

I repeat the pouring process forty-five times exactly. Everybody does it their own way, it depends what you like. Some people actually boil the sauce and pour it, cooked, into the jars. Or you might put some dried hot peppers in with the basil and salt if you want. I make a note to *Canadese*-ize my batch with some savoury spice and maybe some sage at the production end.

"However you like to do it," says Luisa.

Earlier I have a debate with Angelo about when to put the salt in. In his curious way of speaking in the third person he says "my wife" or "she" liked to put the salt into the pails before the sauce went into the jars but Luisa likes to do it this way.

I declare that I will make it Lina's way next year. I don't know if this has an impact on him or if it doesn't have an impact on him; I just don't know, is how I read his face.

"He is still grieving," I say later to Mary, carefully watching him.

I use some leftover 1.5 litre jars for the remaining sauce.

"Why are you using such big jars?" Luisa asks.

I explain that I like to mass produce sauce and give it away to my *Inglese* friends.

"They love me for it and it gives them big stomachs, like me," I say, shrugging my shoulders.

"I see," she says.

Finally, I tip the pail and we fill three-quarters of the last jar. Luisa says she has some sauce inside to fill it all the way, or I can take it home and put it in the fridge but I must use it quickly. I say I will take it home for my daughter Adriana who hates tomatoes but loves tomato sauce. It is the curious culinary logic of children.

I hold the jar up to the light and feel the spirit refract the thick crimson. I take a good, solid drink of it, wipe my mouth on my arm, clap on the lid, and twist it tightly to capture the taste forever.

Luisa goes back into the house and I tightly screw down the lids. We bring the little cart over and place the huge metal pot on it. I carefully load the jars in a circle in the bottom. The sun catches me. I'm it! It is bright now and hot where we are working.

If you put an old tea towel or a football jersey on the bottom of the pot it will keep hot spots from forming and cracking the jars.

There is a debate on how to stack the next layer of jars. Angelo places a small wheel of plywood on the lids of the first layer. There is room on the sides but there is no way the water will boil through the area of the circle.

"Angelo, Angelo don't be such a *testa dura*! The water will never boil in this way. You have to put holes in it. Here, use the cardboard instead," Luisa insists at high volume.

More banter ensues but you can see that Angelo gets the point. He retrieves his plywood wheel and resolutely goes to the yard barn to drill a series of holes in it. Triumphantly he returns and shows his new invention to Luisa. More banter ensues but you can see that she likes his invention. He has improved on the process this year. We place it on top and stack a new layer of jars on it. Angelo and I wheel the cart over to the burner and hoist the metal pot onto it. He turns on the valve of the propane tank and adjusts the pressure with a curious second valve on the hose. Like an old guy who shouldn't be bending down, he bends down and lights the flame with a BBQ lighter. Whoooshhhh!

"Holy mackerel," I say.

Luisa hears us. There is more outrage and banter that *Garibaldi* will kill himself. I tend to agree with her.

"You cannot light the burner that way!" she explains.

Angelo makes a face and waves his hand in a couple of aimless circles like there is too much fuss over nothing.

"She is right, you know," I tell him quietly. I know he knows it.

Come closely, I will tell you a segreto: *These men know when the woman is right but it is not proper to admit it immediately.*

So we do it his way. He adjusts the pressure to the little valve on the hose. I re-light it for him and this time it goes on without a Whoosh! There is the curious sucking sound of propane burning.

The lid is on the pot and I get that deep, contented feeling again.

Angelo explains the purpose of the valve on the line. It was Luisa's husband's device. *Garibaldi* didn't use it last year because he couldn't figure out how it works. But this year he knows how it works and shows me (by turning off the burner) that the second valve regulates the pressure coming out of the tank: by reducing it like so, you can avoid the whooshing sound.

He bends down and demonstrates the lighting process again. There is a pleased, matter-of-fact look on his face: "You see?"

By now Luisa has returned inside. Soon, she is back outside with a tray and plates and a new bottle of wine.

"It is time to eat now," she announces. "Go and wash up in the barrel."

Garibaldi and I stand beside each other and wash up. He looks ancient to me. He is wearing his blue overalls and has a distracted look about him, the kind you get when you are doing repetitive work, not thinking of anything, but when you start to rest, your mind catches up to where your thoughts were. We dry our hands efficiently on a little towel that is always there by the rain barrel and go over to the table. It is in half-shade and we naturally sit where it is cool.

"*Mangia*," I am commanded.

I marvel at a green oval bowl that is filled with crusted zucchini lasagne. There are *pannini*, slightly crisp and still warm, cooked sausages all raggedy at the end and absolutely brilliant. Green beans from the garden and salad with Luisa's oil and vinegar dressing.

We hold hands and say what our children call the Italian prayer: "*Signore benedice questo cibo che stiamo per prendere, cosi sia.*"

When I get to the salad I taste the garlic and something else. It is orégano. I comment and Luisa goes and pulls a small tree from the garden to show me. Exquisite. I must take it home.

"You like to be with old people," she jokes approvingly. "I can't believe how much passion you have to learn."

"That is because I am a rich man," I say. *Garibaldi* looks up for a second like he is remembering something.

The jars rattle away in the pot on the burner and I ask how much time it takes to cook them. Twenty to twenty-five minutes, I am told. In the old days, nobody had watches so they put a potato in with the jars. When the potato was soft it was time to take the jars out. It is another lesson of the Court. You have to be there to learn it.

After dinner, we pile our dishes on trays and Luisa takes them into the house. Angelo and I go stand by the burner. It is time to put the second pot on. He acknowledges this by going to get a small piece of hose. I tell you, you must never, ever throw out an old hose. There are a thousand uses for it. You are a *buffone* if you throw one out. He demonstrates the art of siphoning without using suction because the water is hot and he does not want to scald his mouth. You could use the same technique when you are decanting wine in the cantina but why? We drain off the scalding water from the first pot into the second.

"This saves time," he winks.

"Saving time is *importante*," I say out loud in reply.

We add a bit more water to the second pot, take the first one off and put the new one on the burner. There is another valve adjustment and "*Dio!*" Again, the old guy gets down on his hands and knees and I give him some trouble for it. The fire is lit under the second pot and it will soon start chugging away. Luisa returns to the table, this time with *espresso and biscotti*.

"I lead a charmed life. '*Grazie senora e senore per lezione salsa la scuola*,' " I say. Somehow, they get it.

"You have done everything," Luisa says. "You can go home and now you know how to make it next year. Remember to put the jars upside down on a newspaper. That way you can tell which ones are not sealed."

Together, they walk me out to the car. I have a Mason jar of new mysterious sauce, a bottle of wine from the *cantina*, the orégano and one of my wishes granted. I am—how shall I say it?—complete.

Scene 2.

Variations on Red Peppers.
"The Dance of the Mudcat"

The Italian guy invites the English guy to make peppers

Two days later I get a phone call from *Garibaldi*.
One of the children takes it. "Oh Hi, *Nonno*! Do you want to speak to Mamma?" "Dad, it's *Nonno*. He wants to speak to the *Vagabondo*."

I take the phone. Before I know it I am asked ("If you can make the time, you come") if I am interested in coming down to Luisa's next day to make the peppers. It is a major breakthrough: *incredibile, magnifico!* A—how do I say it?—a *miracolo*. For the first time I am invited to pepper *la scuola* without having to ask. Later I will sing: "*Come prima, piu di prima,* I'm in love" and draw out the word "love" grandly with my outstretched arms.

"What time do you want me there?" I say. "Is it only going to be hard work, because I only like to work hard?"

He asks me politely to come early again, around 8 a.m., so I tell him I will be there just after 7. I shake my head in disbelief and say to Mary, "Wow, they really must have had a great time. I can't believe they actually get it. They know I am interested in being taught."

To turn down an invitation like this would be foolish. It would "violate Rule G" as my father used to say, although he never translated what that phrase meant and I can't remember ever asking him directly. Perhaps it is a Freemason thing because I think Rule G has something to do with the Great Architect, loyalty to family, and how there are certain things or situations that must be done, that you must do, that must occur. Otherwise, you cross the proverbial line and violate Rule G. It makes sense.

The next morning, for some stupid reason, I violate Rule G and sleep in. I find myself racing out the door at 7:05 (*Dio! Stupido!*). Still, there is time to grab a drive-thru coffee; after all, I am an *Inglese (shrug shoulders here)*. I cue up the free jazz of Coltrane, marking time with the beat. I make it to North York and to golden El Dorado by "the forty" which, according to my daughter, translates as 7:40 or twenty to eight.

"I am late!" I say, in stilted English.

Luisa is in the garage and says, "Oh you are here!"

"It is unbelievable. I can't believe it myself. You won't believe it, but I slept in!" I say with mock incredulity.

"You are so funny," says Luisa.

We walk again to the magical shade of the backyard and I see Angelo in his faded blue Toronto Transit Commission overalls tending two old-style barbecues. There are two large boxes of shiny red peppers on the chairs next to him. He puts some little blocks of wood in with the charcoal pieces and he fans the flames.

"You have to get the coals just right. You put them around the grill, like this," he gestures, already into the hard-working cadence of the morning.

"So," I say pausing for effect. "*Il Vagabondo* is here. Thank you for inviting me to pepper *la scuola*. I will not drop out today!"

"Emph," he gestures, tossing his head slightly to suggest he does not believe me. "We'll see," he says.

Luisa immediately launches into a lesson.

"*No, no*, Angelo, you don't do it like that." You don't put the wood in with the charcoal. Now it will burn unevenly. Now we have to wait. You are such a *testa dura!*

"*Dio* Angelo!" I say, mimicking Luisa. "What are you doing? This is wrong!"

"*Eh, eh, eh,*" he says, turning his left hand in dismissive circles like he is waving off flies. "It will be o-kay. Don't be so nervous!"

"*Holy mackerel,*" I say, parroting the phrase I hear him say in the garage when something goes wrong with the wine press, or with the gas burner.

I note that the charcoal pieces must be evenly distributed around the entire circle of the barbecue. You could use briquettes but they use the shards and pieces and that is what I will use, forever.

"Now, I am going to look for an old-style barbecue at a garage sale," I declare to Luisa. "It will be part of my pepper school equipment."

"Write that down," she jokes. "That is one thing that I would like to do is go to garage sales. But I don't need anything and there is never any time to go."

"If you go, you should look for more Mio glasses for me, I say. I am worried that when the last one breaks I will not be able to drink any more *vino*. It will be—*come si dice*—*A grande problemo*." I shrug my shoulders here to over-emphasize the tragic loss.

There is a large barbecue and a smaller, baby one for me.

Luisa declares the fire is ready. She equips each of us with a pair of tongs and a pair of gloves.

"You take the peppers out and prepare them like this on the grill," she instructs.

I take them out and place them with the points facing towards the centre and fan them around the circular grill.

"The key is to not burn them too much. If you burn them too much you cook the pepper and it doesn't taste as good. If you don't get them black (like this), you will have trouble peeling them and then it will take too much time."

"Angelo!" she protests. "This is too black. What are you doing? *Mamma Mia!*" she says, pretending to squabble.

"O-kay, o-kay," he winces, taking the bait on purpose. They peck at each other and I turn the peppers over.

"It is like a foundation on a house," I say referring to the embers. "If you don't build the bottom part successfully, everything above it will be a problem."

"Exactly!" says Luisa. "See, you understand. Good! I will leave you now," she says and disappears into the house.

Angelo and I stand beside each other busy in our work.

Some time passes and I say: "I don't remember you guys ever

making peppers. Did you ever make peppers with Lina, Angelo?"

"No," he says. "We didn't make them."

No elaboration. No conversation. No stories. Just a simple reply to the question. I have learned to marvel at this presence of silence. I come from a family of *yakkers*. At least my Mom was a *yakker* and I like to *yak* and so does my brother.

In the early days I used to complain to Mary. "How come nobody likes to *yak*?" I say. "Lina doesn't *yak*. Angelo doesn't *yak*. Your brother doesn't like to *yak*. You don't like to *yak*. I bet I could spend the entire afternoon down there and nobody would need to say a thing to each other!"

"You don't have to talk to be together," is Mary's logical defence. It takes me years to get it and sometimes I still don't.

Angelo fans his fire to get the flames flaring and the embers burning evenly. I am worried. He is not in the instruction mode. He is deep into the work and deep inside himself getting the work done. I pick up the flattened cornflake box and fan my little barbecue. Angelo nods. I know what to do now and periodically fan both of our fires without any declaration. *Lezione* are everywhere. It is the libretto! The Education, not the Instruction.

We pick the blackened peppers off the grill with tongs and pile the flaccid shapes on a large flat tray. To me they look like mudcat carcasses and I am remembering the men on the shores of the Bay of Quinte in my hometown burning old tires at dusk. The thick black smoke roils out across the water, the long poles go in and mudcat are jigged up and out to flop and flick on shore. I never ate mudcat but now I have a chance to inspect the pepper. You can see them steaming inside where they are cracked. The blackened parts of the skin flake right off in your hand. The smell is strong and mildly nauseous at first. I peel one open and see the seeds, the steaming juice and the fibrous inside. I plop it back on the tray and return to my pepper turning. Angelo shows me how to stand them up on their end to get the tops blackened.

"You don't want to waste anything," he says.

It is so—how do you say it?—perfect how the peppers stand right up on their ends like that. The stems hook through the grill grating and it is easy to get ten or so standing up like old, bent red men in the *piazza*. When they are ready you remove them with tongs and stack them.

It is another *bella giornata*. The shade retreats around the corner to rest under the patio umbrella. The barbecues are in the sun now. Our eyes get teary when the wind shifts the smoke towards us. We are intent upon our task. I get the enchanted feeling again. I know exactly where I am now. Everything within my gaze is the way it should be. I feel the Order. I feel all the backyard systems going quietly about their business, doing what they are supposed to do. It is all strangely sensual and even now, the air exudes a kind of masculinity and femininity as if I can tell which of the beans are guys and which of the tomatoes are girls. I laugh to myself. You have to be crazy to be an *Inglese* in *Garibaldi's* Court but I have my timeless lesson now and I really know what *contento* means. It is a gift.

Finally, the last pepper is blackened to perfection. Angelo picks it off the grill with his tongs and places it on the tray. There is a quiet, unspoken sense of accomplishment as we gaze at our heap of pepper carcasses. You can see the steam crudely gasping out like some of them are passing wind.

"Angelo!" I tease. "Why do you not cook this one properly?" I say, pointing to a pepper in the middle of the pile. "*Dio!*"

"I-don't-know," he replies, distractedly and in a sing-song voice.

I can tell he is thinking ahead to the next step. Luisa comes back outside through the sliding doors. Her timing is perfect. She carries a couple of platters, two knives, two more metal salad bowls and two bananas.

"I will teach you the next step now," she announces, "but first you have something to eat." There is time to do a little more work and then we will eat lunch.

"Are you still enjoying yourself?" she asks.

"*Si, io sono molto contento*" I reply as if I have been making the peppers for years. She smiles.

After the *frutta* is eaten, Luisa sits down beside us at the table and picks out a pepper. She places it on the platter and begins pulling off the blackened skin. It flakes off easily but there are some parts where the skin is still attached.

"This is why the fire must be right," she says, "Otherwise you waste time."

I see the lesson now. If the embers are right and as much of the pepper is as black as possible, the skin slips right off. Where it is still red or green, the skin adheres and the scraping begins. Luisa picks up a knife with a serrated edge and begins scraping the outside of the pepper. The skin is stubborn but it comes off.

"If you leave the skin on, the peppers won't taste as good," she tells me again.

With her fingers, she creates a seam and gently but deliberately opens up the pepper. Carefully she peels away the skin from the stem and core area at the top. The hot juice and seeds sluice onto the plate and she removes the seed pod with her thumb. The pepper skin is now opened up fully and fanned out onto the platter. You push the seeds and outside skin to the edge of the plate. With your knife you start scraping and scraping and scraping. Finish off the outside, flip it over and finish off the inside making sure to get all the seeds out. You cut away any little black marks on the pepper to make it presentable. I like to cheat and cut off the curled parts at the top of the pepper when they are being stubborn and won't be cleaned. You can pop them into your mouth and not even break stride. I comment that the completed pepper now looks exactly like a smoked salmon carcass. Luisa picks hers up and lays it in the salad bowl.

"Here is the last step," she instructs.

She picks up the flesh like a cloth and begins tearing it into thin strips. It depends how you like to do it but she puts her portions into little baggies and freezes them. "When company comes, you pull one out, thaw it, add some oil and a little garlic, some parsley and you always have something good to eat," she announces looking pleased.

I look over at Angelo and I can see that his mind is off again in the place that hard work has taken it for generations. I skin my first pepper under approving eyes and when it is done I hold it up: "Ahh, *perfetto!* Luisa! This one is a *Caravaggio.*" The next one is a *Fra Angelico* and by the time I get to the *Botticelli*, Luisa is sure that I have understood.

She gets up from the table and goes back into the house. I reach for a mudcat and soon I am taken to the same place as *Garibaldi*. I concentrate on the task. It doesn't take long for my thoughts to drain off like the seeds and the juice, onto the platter. I scrape them into another bowl and enjoy the metallic scratch of the knife edge on porcelain. About ten peppers in, the tedium takes over and I enter the thoughtless trance of repetitive work. The universal language where there is absolutely no need to say anything. The day is warm. The neighbour's dog is barking. A jet flies over en route to the airport. There are two heaping trays of peppers that must be cleaned and opened and scraped. It is not time to eat. Like a seagull gliding by overhead, a wish dives across my thoughts and I want my children to be here, to know and to feel what I am learning. I reach automatically now for another pepper, pull the brittle blackened skin off with my bare hands, scrape, pull it open and scrape again. Inspect, onto the pile, pluck a few errant seeds out of the bowl with the tip of my knife, scrape the plate, stand up, stretch and dump the contents into the compost: re-load.

"It is time to stop working. We are going to eat now," Luisa announces at noon.

Angelo is still not back from his journey, but together, stiffly we amble over to the water barrel to wash our hands. The water is so cool and I cup it and rub it over my face and neck just like he does.

"It is time to eat now," he says and I can't quite read whether he is happy or sad or even fully present. Old guys get that way sometime. I know if I try to ask him now what he is thinking, I will be shrugged away.

"*La bella tavola!*" I announce grandly and exhaust my linguistic repertoire.

"It is nothing," Luisa replies.

I pour some wine into my Mio glass, top up Angelo's and gesture to Luisa. "*Poco poco vino, senora?*" Luisa declines, saying she prefers *aqua* after her meal. Gently, we hold hands and say the Italian prayer.

"*Grazie per lezione pepe la scuola,*" I say.

"*Chin chin,*" says Angelo.

"*Buon appetito!* You must be hungry; have some pizza," Luisa says, passing me the tray.

"*Io sono in paradiso,*" I say.

Homemade pizza, lightly crusted and topped with onion, cheese, peppers and zucchini. Why, they are the first batch of peppers we made! The *Caravaggio*, the *Angelico*, the *Botticelli* bathed in oil and herbs and prepared in a narrow white dish. More sausages, more bread, more salad, more *vino*. More, more!

Our talk takes us first to the old country during the war when it was hard. Then the stories set sail for Toronto and the early life there. Each tale is lifted off the tray of memory, told and stacked to be frozen back in time: the first job putting tomatoes in trays and wrapping them in cellophane. The girls in the factory, the mean ones who used to call us names. The British war bride who was older than the other girls, she was so nice.

"They used to ask us to work weekends and even though it was overtime, none of the other girls wanted to do it. But we were glad to do it. It was a struggle and we made do with what we had," Luisa says.

"And this is why we are the way we are now," she concludes, breaking the reverie to bring us all back to the table and the cement patio stones, the bright sun causing us to huddle in the shade.

Luisa gets up and begins to collect the plates.

I say *scuzzi* and head down to the *cantina*; that is, the wonderful *Inglese* root cellar, to refill the bottle of wine from the gallon container. It is perched on clean two-by-fours underneath wooden shelving, made from the solid ends of wine cases: Dutch Boy Carrignane, Sapore Dolce, Ballantine, E Dolce, L Bar L and Ma-Ma-Mia! with the picture of the *signora* dressed up like a *signorina* in the corner. (Her dress is definitely in need of—how do I say it?—supervision.)

There is a beautiful musty smell down here. *Dio!* How do I explain this space to you? It is so sacred. All the *cantinas* are different but this one runs along the front of the house along the foundation on the inside wall. It is cold in there, not freezing but chilly enough to keep everything nice. Benches and shelves run the entire length of the foundation and along the interior wall that separates it from the warm basement. They are stocked with gallon jugs of *vino*, the Brio, the Mio, maybe a couple of fifty-gallon drums, smaller twenty-litre containers, green demijohns and plenty of clear plastic tubing for the siphoning. There are cases of homemade tomato sauce, the paste, onions and garlic drooping on nails, nuts, canned chick peas, and things I have yet to discover. Tucked in the corner is a container of sour wine vinegar, pungent when you take off the lid and dip your finger inside to taste. I am enchanted every time I set foot in there.

But for now, I remove the plastic tube from the hole in the top of the lid on the burgundy gallon jug. I take a long, hard pull of the contents (to get the siphon going). Slowly, agelessly, the wine bottle, pressed into service when its contents of rye were finished, fills to just below the brim. I pull the tube up above the gravity line and expertly twist the cap onto the bottle with one hand. A last, long pull on the tube and I replace it back into the lid on the jug. The happy task complete, I go out through the basement, up the stairs and resume my place at the table and pour a last one for *Garibaldi* and for me. Luisa leaves and comes back with a tray of fruit.

"You have done everything now," Luisa begins the familiar phrase. "You know the—how do you say it?—the process." You have helped us so much and if you want to go downtown to buy *la musica*, you can go now."

Earlier in the morning I told Angelo and Luisa that I was going to pepper school and then downtown to buy music, probably Coltrane. It is an old joke with Angelo and his wife, my mother-in-law Lina, and I. I always say that I am going to buy *la musica* and I ask Angelo if, when he was a boy, his father gave him money to go to the tobacconist to buy CDs and other important things. This inevitably provokes a happy problem and a playful argument.

"Ha! Do you think we had the money for that?" (*make a circling motion with your left hand here and translate it as a sign of mock disbelief that anyone could have the frivolous luxury of buying music, like it was something you actually needed.*)

In my mind, like sauce school, I thought I will be done by two-ish and still have some of the day left to roam. It is not to be and this is important for you to know. It takes more time to make the peppers than it does to make the sauce. Forget about buying music. With a heaping tray and a half of mudcat sitting on the table by the house, you can see that we will be lucky to be done by early evening.

Now, fully rested, we return to our trays and our knives and our scraping platters. Coaxed by the languid glow of the *vino*, it is easy for us to fall back into our work-trance. After ten more peppers I come to.

"Angelo!" I say in the spirit of improvisation. "We must have music! How can we work so hard and not have music? Surely you had the stereo going when you were working in the fields. Surely you had the music when you were feeding Rosie and the pigs?"

At the mention of Rosie, I see him perk up and tug at his memory as the slow gait of the family mule ambles across his face. Rosie suddenly reappeared one Christmas in the Nativity scene at the base of the tree, with a little wooden sign around her neck, tied with a golden thread. She towers above the sheep and the camels, witness to the celebration of the birth of *Jesu*.

By now, Luisa is outside again. She hears my call for the music and announces she will get the portable stereo.

"Luisa," I say, "bring the Abruzzi one."

Soon the rough authentic folk songs of the Alan Lomax Treasury of Italian Music provide a backdrop to our pepper ballet. The songs are remarkably like the wine: rough, primitive, full bodied, filled with presence. *Al fresco*, a symphony of the shade! Songs of love, of death, of shepherds and lost sheep found.

I can tell they are enjoying the music and I am reminded of *Garibaldi's* story. It was impossible for the boys and the girls to meet and the only way to do that was to go to town, to the *piazza* and mill about. Someone there had an old wind-up Victrola, with a small bell speaker and one record. One of the boys would wind up the stereo and suddenly there was music and clapping and dancing all coming to life under the stars. Slowly, the rhythmic breath is expended and again revived to shouts and laughter and more singing. "This was how we passed time. We had to make our own fun," he says to me.

When the songs of Abruzzi finish, it is mid-afternoon. Luisa goes into the house to rest. I get up to stretch and see what other CDs are around. Because it is the only thing she has, I put on Andrea Bocelli to maintain the *fresco*, knowing immediately I will regret it. Ersatz-opera. "Cur-ses," as my mother would say. It is "too much of a muchness!" What we need is Zinca, or Maria, or Giuseppe di Stefano. I make a note to expand their opera repertoire, noting it can be a gift this holiday season from Rosie, for the man who needs nothing.

After ten more mudcats, we finish one tray and move well onto the second. It is very hot now and talking takes too much energy.

Restlessly, the Bocelli plays out and I rescue the fading weary ambiance with John Coltrane's "The Bethlehem Years." Soon the air is painted with jazz, stacks of flesh-red mudcat, the clank of metal on porcelain, *Garibaldi* and Me. There is nothing finer. I sing the libretto written for this day alone. It makes me laugh. I feel the gaiety I sometimes observe in Italian men being silly, so out of stoic character, a little embarrassing but funny to watch, particularly with the ones they love.

By now, it is the height of the hot-time. We are tired. In dialect we call it *stango*. I tell Angelo I will be seeing peppers in my dreams tonight. He laughs. We hear the sliding door open and look up. On time, in time, like the rising and traverse of the sun across a North York sky, like a system, Luisa presents us with a tray—some *biscotti* and a pot of *espresso*.

"It is time to stop now," she announces.

No quarrel here. We set aside the scraping platters and make room for the tiny cups with clearance to pour. A stretch, an amble to the water barrel to wash up, and soon we are back at the table, together.

"You have helped so much," says Luisa. "Last year, Angelo only had one box and he still had half to do by this time. If you want to go now, you can go."

"*Signora*, I cannot go until the work is done," (*shrug shoulders here*) I say in my serious *Inglese/Italian* cadence, minus the actual translation, of course. "You know that this is the true *lezione*."

"The young," she says. "They don't usually show this much interest."

"I am older than I look," I reply.

The taste of espresso is everything to me. I prefer it without sugar and I always need to restrain myself from gulping it down like water. I pour a second and go to pour a third. The pot is empty.

"I could make more," Luisa offers.

"No, I am content. Thank you," I say.

"*Prego*," she says.

We collect the cups and place them on the tray. There is a slight breeze. The afternoon begins to dance with the earliest part of the evening. The end is in sight and we know we will finish the peppers in another hour or so.

As Luisa gets up to go back into the house I say, "Luisa, don't go.

Look how much I have done compared to Angelo. He is ruthless. He is a *testa dura*. He makes me do all the scraping and then claims it for himself!"

We all laugh and then resume our work.

Because we are near the end there is no work-trance. There is time to make up a lesson of my own. *La Lezione del Vagabondo*! I explain it to Angelo.

"You see, Angelo. When you love someone you do not always take the black peppers even though you want to. No, you take a black pepper and then you take a not-so-black pepper so the other guy is not always scraping away. I am worried that you are always taking the black peppers. What do you think?"

"You are right," he says happily.

For some strange reason, it seems important to me that I leave the last pepper for *Garibaldi* to finish. It is the same reason that the first-born son should receive the wine press when the father is no longer using it. Like everything else there is a system of respect that must be tilled and planted in little rows, watered, tended and, above all, harvested. Deep down I know this.

"I cannot believe we are done," I say, arching my back.

As we start to clear away the tools of the day, my wife suddenly arrives with our children and my son's friend. They have been shopping. Another wish is granted.

"I didn't know if you would be done or not, but I decided we would come anyway," Mary laughs.

Daughter and grandchildren kiss *Garibaldi* and he glows with happiness. More kisses.

I know what he knows. It is not at all about the peppers. Peppers are a means to an end.

Luisa hears the noise and comes out to greet her guests. Immediately, the children are offered orange pop and chips and before we know it, we have cleaned and wiped down the patio table. Once again we dine al fresco on leftover pizza squares, a few sausages, the "Three Peppers" in oil, bread, melon, nuts and wine.

Later, we are walked out to the cars, our children are divided for company and I am travelling north on the highway with *mia figlia*, Adriana.

"Did you have a good day, Dad?" she asks.

"Adriana, did you know that there is poetry in every day?" I reply, slightly distracted.

"Yes, Dad," she says.

"You can compose, live and sing with it, if you want to. It is … like squeezing the remaining juice out of the *mosto*, you will always find something," I say.

"Were you in a poem today, Daddy?" She asks.

"Exactly!" I say, driving north into the stars.

Scene 3.

Dinner *al Fresco*

A typical meal

The following week, Mary and I make a successful attempt to eat dinner with Angelo and Luisa. We arrive at 5:30 ("at the thirty") with the children in tow.

"*La famiglia Vagabondo* is here!" I announce while strolling down the laneway to the cement patio at the back of the house.

"Angelo! Maria is here!" I hear Luisa call out.

Angelo ambles to the door of his apartment. He looks healthy. He is happy that we have arrived.

"Hel-lo!" he says.

"Hi, *Nonno!*" say the kids in unison. There are kisses all around. Next in line is Mary. "Hi, Daddy!" she says giving him a big hug.

Next, it is my turn.

"So," I say. "I am back. I am worried that I left the peppers and all of the sauce with you and now it is gone."

"You are right," he says matter-of-factly. "There is no food here, you can go back home now."

"*Buona serra, signora!*" I say, ignoring him. "You see? I had such a good time, you cannot get rid of me!"

"That is true!" Luisa replies.

The children disappear to watch TV and drink orange pop. Angelo, Maria and I go to the patio table to inspect the huge Michelin map of

Italy. Luisa is in the kitchen. In a few days they will depart on a seniors' tour of Portugal, Spain, southern France and Italy. It looks to be a religious pilgrimage of sorts with stops at St. Anthony of Padua's Shrine, the Sanctuary of Alcobaca, the Basilica of Our Lady of Pilar, Lourdes, Monte Carlo (!), Ponte Vecchio in Florence and the Vatican. They will leave the tour in Rome and take the bus to Boiano. Here, they will be picked up by his sister and brother-in-law, my friends from last year, and they will be whisked up the impossible back roads to Castropignano.

"There you will drink *benezene* and play *scopa* in the *piazza*!" I say to him, definitively.

It is his first return to the Hometown and the second time travelling without his wife Lina, who died three and a half years ago.

He has lived as a tenant at 22 El Dorado for the past year and a half. He pays rent. Luisa is his landlady and together they are "companions" who share each other's company. They do things together and return life to the approximate order in which it used to be, like the systems of the garden. It is an alternately modern and ancient arrangement, for they are not companions of the bed but companions of the life. I know there is a huge *lezione* here but it does not come all at once. There are so many of my generation who choose not to learn it but frankly, what are you going to do? He is happy, so I am happy. It is foolish to argue with the weather. If it rains, you watch it. If it is sunny you find the shade.

"You will not die from this," was my mother-in-law's constant *lezione*. She is right. Mary and I are not dying.

"So what if it's hard," Mary says to me, referring to her grief. "It is not going to change anything."

I tell *Garibaldi* that he is like a corn plant in a field the year following the harvest. No matter what the crop, no matter what the field, or if the field is fallow that year, there are always one or two plants left over from the season before, growing tall despite the odds.

"Go and look in the field for yourself," I tell him. "I am smarter than I look." Way smarter because I, *Il Vagabondo*, have married a corn plant! It is—how do you say it?—my good fortune.

We touch Villavallelonga on the map in relation to Castropignano and I declare that I will come with them. I call for an atlas to locate the cities in Portugal and Spain and trace the route through Nice. Luisa brings a globe. Lina used to do the same thing and I get silly again.

"*Dio*! Luisa, you are not leaving the planet are you?" I say.

"No, it is too expensive," she replies.

In time the map is folded. We make arrangements to take them to the airport on Saturday at exactly 2:30 to meet the rest of the tour. The sun leaves the patio area and its heat starts to give way. A tablecloth replaces the thick plastic on the table. Maria goes to help with the meal and I take the bottle down to the *cantina* to start the siphon going. I watch the rosy level rush up through the neck and pinch off the tube in the nick of time! It is an art. When I return, the dishes are stacked on the table and the food is arriving. It is nothing, really. Grilled chicken breast, what looks to be a boiled pork shoulder, glistening green beans, mudcat-*Caravaggio*, bread, salad and dressing boosted with orégano, oil and vinegar. Wine for me and my wife and—how do you say it?—Sprite for the kids. It is everything, really, and the time passes beautifully. After some melon and chocolate the *bambini* are excused and we remove the plates. It is dusk now so we usher in the cool evening under the umbrella, sipping *espresso* and talking about important things.

Garibaldi and Lina are my role models of love. They were so happy after forty-nine years of marriage that it was like springtime around them. They quietly went about their own routines and they were connected. It was as if an imaginary sun was between them and the sheer warmth of it constantly turned their gaze towards the centre. The first lump appeared on her neckline where the silver chain of the crucifix rested naturally on her shoulder bone. Another one pops up and two years later we watch them load her coffin into a vault that her sister-in-law calls "the apartments." Extremely efficient: crank up the dolly, load her in, caulking guns come out: *click-clack, click-clack, click-clack*. Beautiful bead and the guy spreads it with a little putty knife. Face plate lifted on, the screws go in and the two men discreetly pack up to disappear around the corner. *Addio*.

"If you are having any troubles I want you to come to me," *Garibaldi* once tells me in the garage and I appreciate his gesture of protection.

"Did you go through any rough times, Angelo?" I ask him, back in the early days when we smoked his Export A's with complete abandon.

"Yes," he says in his gentle, innocent, completely undefended way. "I was mad at my wife and my family for ten years once. I would come home and then go out. I didn't talk to them. I was always so nervous."

"A decade is a long time!" I say, shocked. "How did you come out of it?"

"One day I woke up and I kept saying to myself, 'Angelo! You are wrong to be so mad all the time. They are not doing anything wrong.' From then on, it was better and my life is happy now. We still fight and she is stubborn but it doesn't last. We are always laughing." He told me that the neighbours say they are like newlyweds.

It grows softly dark around the table now. I see the light from the TV beating its languid strobe in the house. We barely see each other's faces. The talk somehow shifts to widowhood and the crushing pain of living alone when your spouse dies. Luisa's husband was a "bookman," an engineer who played the piano and loved music. He was younger than she was and she used to tease him about being a boy. "Ha!" he would say. "You think they know more than I know, but you are wrong," was his defiant reply.

"He told me I should not worry after he dies, that I should look after myself," Luisa says quietly.

"Besides, you should know that I will be happy in heaven and I will marry a foreign girl and she will massage my feet."

There is a respectful quiet that is punctuated by "that was our life" and something else which I miss.

We talk of family and the unhappy grudges between mothers and daughters, between sons and fathers, brothers and sisters, sisters-and brothers-in-law. It is cooler now. We grow tired yet there is an urgency in the night—an urgency to be known, to set down the eternal burden of despair and then, to rest.

Yet, in the dark, if only for a moment, my demons appear. My enchantment fades, ridden away on bloody wisps of grief across a field of scorn.

"Family is everything. I doubt it," I snarl to myself. The umpteenth Italian function I have been to and all they ever say is 'We never see each other any more except at funerals and weddings.' They are like everyone else. They get angry with each other. They hold grudges. Like my friend at work. He married an English girl, but his wife is still a witch to his mamma. The old *nonna* can't even be invited to her grandson's wedding, a generation after the fact. She is so nervous. Time passes, letters are written, family intermediaries sought, and still my friend and his *strega* and their children are dead to her. Jesus Christ! (*Help us all*)

"I can see that you still care so much for Frank and that you miss him, Luisa," I say gently in the soft night, my enchantment returning unharmed. "I understand. It is the same with Angelo and Lina, they are my—*come si dice?*—my role models. My heroes. I hope Maria and I can be that way when we are old."

"That is why you go so well together—you are a ... good match," Luisa tells me kindly.

"It is such a waste, to stay mad, to never be able to forgive," I conclude, sensing the mood is shifting and we are growing weary. "Life is too short."

Still, it is an urgency of youth and the useless ways of demons to repossess and before they flutter off, I am back in my mind at the kitchen table now. It is late. I am angry. We are in *Garibaldi's* Court. There is a problem in the family. It happens everywhere. The usual— how do you say it?—argument. I appeal to the grand patriarch to solve it, to lay down the law with his people.

"You should say something," I say accusingly like a *hothead*, smacking the table for emphasis.

"You should not be so nervous," he says tenderly covering my hands. "When we were back home, before we came here we used to say, 'If you move the compost it will stink.' And that is why we say nothing." He says it resolutely and looks at me straight through both eyes into my soul so I get it. It is one of the few times I see him pound the table with the palm of his hand and it drives off my demons. I feel bad. Perhaps I am the one who stinks.

Luisa and *Garibaldi* are stirring now. Maria sighs the way her mother sighed and begins to gather the *espresso* spoons. The clack of cups stacked on saucers signals the end of this silent nativity of friendship, this field-mass *al fresco*, and without glancing at our watches we all know it is time to go home. Something has grown between us the way the zucchini suddenly looks *grande* the next morning. I found another lesson. There is a time to talk and a time to stop talking. It is different from the distracted silence of repetitive work in the sun. Standing, stretching, we gather up our children wordlessly; there are kisses and we are walked out along the laneway to our car.

"*Ciao*, Luisa! *Ciao, Garibaldi!*" I say dramatically. "We will be here at exactly 1:13 p.m. on Saturday to take you to the *aeroporto. Arrivedello!* Luisa! Do you know that is how they teach you to say goodbye in Italian night school. I never heard anyone say *arrivedello* in my life. I am not saying it right on purpose. *Dio!* It is—*come si dice?*—stupid!"

"You are so funny," she laughs.

"Angelo, make sure you pack your cane, and remember—there is no rush. Let the vacation come to you, don't run after it and everything will be fine."

"I know, I know," he says happily.

As we glide north on Highway 400, the kids are sprawled in the back with their headphones on, dreamy, being led like sheep to bed the way children do when they are tired and they know their parents are content.

"Mary," I say, "translate your Dad's saying for me: If you move the compost it will stink."

"*Se sposti il composto puzza.*"

"Tonight was just like peeling the skin off peppers," I say as we fly silently past another car. "It flakes right off and then you throw it all in the compost."

"Yes, but keep your feet out of it," she laughs and grabs my arm.

Act II

[Act II]

Scene 1.

Hometown *Aria*

Reflections on seeing the old guy's Hometown

When Angelo and Luisa return from Europe, I realize that Mary and I would have lost much treasure if we had not taken the children to Italy to see their grandparents' Hometown. We went three years after Lina died, and I think *Garibaldi* went back because we did.

I declared as much and more to Angelo late one evening at the kitchen table after he moved to Luisa's. It is another—how do they call it in their language?—*veglia*. We are sitting up, remembering.

"I can't believe it," I say. "In Castropignano, you always seem to be walking up. Even when you are walking down, you are walking up! I am sure I lost twenty pounds there, although Luisa, you will not be able to tell it now," I add, patting my belly.

"Well, if you are hungry, you eat," she says shrugging her shoulders.

The lines of North York shrink quickly. They grow smaller and smaller, fading until a sudden burst of white cloud turns our gaze. We are retrieved in Rome at the Mercure Accor Hotel, Piazza Bologna by Emanuelle, a handsome young driver known to and arranged through Barbara, *Garibaldi's* niece. We drive east three or so hours. From the base of the valley, I look up to see the shining stone of the *Castillo*, proud ruins on the uppermost part of the town, set like a jewel in a clean blue sky. We are taken to the *piazza*, around the corner and down, stopping at the cascade of steps that lead past the little street to the house of Biagio and Nina, Angelo's youngest sister. Emanuelle efficiently deposits our red Canadian luggage. He has a word with Biagio and before I say goodbye, he is gone. Barbara has made excellent arrangements and it has all run smoothly. I am left with a vague feeling of importance. The *Americanos* from Toronto have arrived. The town is remarkably empty and I barely see anyone standing up to the bright afternoon sun that has already made its presence known on the back of my neck. We are shown the refurbished *casa* where we will be staying for six days. I am given the key and Biagio carefully instructs us on the lock mechanism. The door opens to brown tile and lemon yellow Mediterranean walls. The stairs curve up to the right past an outcrop of rock pushing through the wall. A kitchen, a gas stove, a large dining table and some chairs. Steep stairs continue left up to the third floor and there we find a bathroom and two bedrooms. A doorway leads outside to the roof; the area is half rocks and half roof. Eventually, we are led back down to the first floor to another cool back room built amidst the stone. There is a fridge and Biagio opens it.

Arranged neatly are bottles of wine, Nastro Azzurro '*benezene*', milk, half a melon, jars of olives and sauce, cheese and some other pickled things that I do not recognize. That *cantina* smell is in the air. I start to relax. "*Grazie,*" is all I can tumble out. I try to mean every intention of it by saying it through my eyes. This is the big leagues. The Hometown. These are *la famiglia Garibaldi*. My wife was born here. The burning bush.

Maria explains that we have some time to rest and clean up. Then we are to go next door to her grandparents' house to eat and to meet everyone.

I go down to review the contents of the fridge again, while the children claim their beds and dressers and Maria begins to open the suitcases and set up our system. I follow suit by inspecting the bathroom and the kitchen area, pausing again on the stairs to rub my hand over the rough rock outcrop, which stands in place of the wall. Everything is sculpted out of rock, through the rock, around the rock and within the rock. It is delightful. The sun-yellow walls, the sparse furniture, the rich hardwood floor, the solid brown steps, the dresser drawers filled with linen. The entire place feels smartly dress casual and I try it on for the first time. It is new, stiff and clean and I know already it will become a favourite in my wardrobe. The *piazza* seems to fit me this way and I cannot wait to try on the *Castillo*.

After a time, we are called next door to dinner. Gingerly, we close the front door and I try the key for the first time. The lock clicks and we pass through a little courtyard to climb up a flight of steep stone steps nearby. We part a beaded curtain and our eyes adjust to the relative darkness of the kitchen. The reflex of aroma through nose to stomach is immediate for we are going to dinner in *Garibaldi's* father's house-in-town.

At the head of the table is Biagio Giambattista. We are introduced to his family, all bustling within the happy motion of their routines. There is Salvatore and Marica and their children Noemi, Gabriele and Ester. Enrica and Enzo and their *bambini*: Valentina and Kristina. Later we will meet daughter number three, Barbara and her dashing companion Graziano from Naples. Giovanina (Nina) is at the stove. I say everyone's name phonetically a thousand times over, pledging to get them right. When your Italian is so impoverished, the least you can do is get the names right and the rest will come later.

"*Buonasera*," I say and there is much laughter and giggling.

The teens, Valentina and Kristina, are learning English in school and Biagio knows and will attempt English-in-sentences with a twinkle in his eye. It is Barbara who is fluent and later I will be relieved to talk to her. I will ask her to tell her father how much of a pleasure it is to meet him, that his family is so beautiful, that they all must come to Toronto and that my family is changed forever by meeting them.

But for now, I must rely, when I am feeling bold and independent on my Berlitz "if you speak English you can speak Italian" Self-Teacher book. Of course, all other times we stick like glue to *mia moglie*, whose name in her country-of-birth has reverted so easily back to Maria.

The mysterious dual names of Italian women intrigue me. Angie is *Angeolina*, Lina is *Pasqualina*, Lucy is *Lucia*, Phyllis is *Filomena*, Rose is *Rosa*, Mary is *Maria* (*hold your arms out like you are in love*). It is—how do I say it?—so *romantica*!

"He does not speak Italian?" I hear Nina ask Maria.

"No," she says simply and with a grin.

"*Io sono Italiano notte la scuola ... come si dice? ...* drop-out," I say with mock pride.

There are puzzled looks.

Maria laughs and slaps me on the arm. In Italian she tells them how early in our marriage I signed up for Italian lessons in North York. It was every Wednesday night. On the second Wednesday, the students are asked to explain their ideal meal. "Ah, *Dio*" I say. "*La tassa, carne, polo, pane, insalate, vino e espresso...*"

"*Que e la tassa?*" The instructor asks with a grin. The entire class turns to me now.

"You know, *la tassa*," I say again. "When you are boiling water for the pasta just before it is ready, you ladle out some of the hot water with one or two of the *penne rigate* in it and add as much homemade red wine as you want. You bring the bowl up to your nostrils and breathe in and this helps clear you out if you have a cold. Then you drink it."

"I never heard of it!" the instructor laughs.

By now the entire class is laughing. Several stand up and point their finger at me and place their hands over their mouths.

"He is an idiot," I hear someone whisper.

The next thing you know I am fighting the entire class.

"So after that," I say, finishing Maria's story in English, "I told them there is no point in being here, they don't know what *la tassa* is. How could they teach me anything? So I dropped out and never went back—But!" I say raising my index finger instructively while tilting my head to the left with a practiced shrug, "I returned to a different school a decade later to graduate with my little Italian Conversation certificate 'Part one', tourist class."

Maria translates and there is laughter. *Il Vagabondo*, the—how do you call it?—the Jester. The *burlone*.

By now the meal is ending. Our children decline thirds and the other kids take them out into the tiny courtyard to catch lizards. Later there are screeches and we all step out to see the scorpion. Blackish red, sharp and oily, my first reaction is to crush it. I am surprised at how small it is. Rather than crush it, the children play with it by moving it around with sticks and screaming.

Later in the week, I will behold a three-act play starring a large slug, a toothpick crucifix and some tomato sauce. I note that there is a complete lack of shiny bicycles, pogo sticks, skateboards, plastic cars you sit in and push with your feet, and for the life of me, I can't see any Star Wars space ships or Jurassic Park raptors lurking in the corners. No one is playing catch. Instead, there is the annual *Ferragosto* soccer tournament. It is the holiday-time when everyone leaves the city to go and relax. My son *Nico* is pressed into volunteering by his cousin Kristina and before he knows it, he is playing in the games with the boys and the men, on the pitch around the corner, by the monument and the large *piazza*. Later we play *scopa* in the small *piazza*, opposite the *cantina* with *Zio* Domenico and Cousin Nicola. A group of young men walk up and enter the corner of my eye.

"Nicholas! Nico!" One of them calls out in a sonorous voice. A commemorative medallion is placed into the palm of my son's hand by a handsome looking young guy. It reads "*Triangolare Di Calcio Castropignano.*"

"*Grazie,*" Nick says, with a shy grin.

"Nick!" I say. "Now you have an adventure to tell *Nonno*. He will be so proud."

We continue our card playing and like a cat swiping the mouse, *la bella setta* (the beautiful seven) is thrown down with a flourish and my partner Nicola takes the trick.

"Bravo, Nicola. *Excellente!*" I say.

This game over, I lean back in my chair, take a sip of *benezene* and watch men smoking and laughing in clusters while children scoot up narrow stone streets for parts unknown. It is all *al fresco*. The sun stomped away in a huff and the shadows softly mix the air. The enchantment sets in.

"At that time," *Garibaldi* says to me, "there was no money for the toys. We used to make our own fun. We used to go into town and just go around. There was always something."

I picture his face remembering. The thoughts sweep across his features and later he shows me how to make a ball out of an old gray stocking.

"Here. That was our soccer ball!" he says triumphantly.

***

We are walking now with Nina and she takes us up the narrow street, past the *posta* building and the store where you can buy meat. Up we go over the rise and disappear down another little street. The wooden doors still have little round holes at the bottom to let the cats in and out. We pass houses newly renovated and not yet moved into. They stand next to comfortable, flowering, well lived-in homes. And beside them, it is not unusual to see derelict abandoned houses of bones with socketless windows and rubble and beams crashed down on floors. Beside that and through those beads is a variety store, I think. Nina goes in and comes out with a key to the place next door. An old woman sneaks a look at us through the window. I smile and wave. In a moment we are inside a little museum. It is two or three rooms packed with artefacts and tools and memories of old days. It is like having some of your dreams filled in as if they are a work-in-progress. Over here is the canvas, some detailed sketches in thin pencil suggest a scene but over here, here is where the subject is taking shape in glorious colour. The fine details, the realism in the magic of old stories presented to view. I see a wall of crocks and porcelain plates. Huge wooden bowls and spoons, wooden pitch forks and an old wine press. Cans of poisonous mosquito spray. A wall full of keys and the machine that makes them. Shoes cobbled by hand. A huge stone pulled by horses to flatten the grain. The machine that crushes the *cane* so you can strip it into fibre and make coarse linen from it. We have the entire place to ourselves and Nina takes her time to tell us what it all means.

"Nina! You are our—*come si dice?*—our *molto bene tour guida*" I say, happily. "Just like Barbara." Barbara, her middle daughter, is the authentic tour organizer who will later take us to the island of Capri. Her *amico* Graziano, my new Neopolitan friend, will have the pole position passing Mount Vesuvius, around the bend and all the way to the flat lands of Pompeii.

"You drive faster in reverse than I do in fifth gear!" I will later say when we just miss a car deep in the laneways of Naples. Barbara will translate and Graziano will look pleased.

"*Si*," Nina simply says, smiling happily, somehow understanding what I want to say.

We leave the store and return the key to the old woman next door.

"*Grazie, signora,*" I say, feeling brave. "*Io sono Canadese. Mia moglie e Italiana da Castropignano. Figlia di Angelo Molinaro.*"

"*Si,*" she nods with the worried look that strangers sometimes get. The same look that I got from Lina when I first started coming around.

We walk up again, through more laneways to what appears to be the crest of the hill. My knees feel the incline. It is hard to know where the crest is because the houses are so close and the streets, so narrow. Castropignano is a dream. There is no sense of time or space here. The town could hold eleven hundred people or eleven thousand and you would never know it. Through the stairways I sense that we are making our way along a street on the outside of town. We happen upon a woman who is in her late fifties. She recognizes Nina and soon they are in a happy singsong greeting, speaking urgently to one another.

"*Oh si!*" she says looking over at us and there are kisses as Maria is introduced first and then me. The older woman holds on to Maria and strokes her arm with affection. She is making sure that her dream is real and I am told that this woman's mother prepared the wedding cake for the feast when *Garibaldi* and my mother-in-law were married in 1951. Maria blinks and rubs her eyes. Nina looks delighted. I feel tall and strangely loyal. It is an elemental loyalty, primitive and instinctual, awakening deep in my Anglo-Irish heritage on the Adrian Robert McLaren side. I feel like I would do anything to make this woman's life happier, anything, anytime—like she is family—and suddenly, I feel embarrassed by the passion within.

"I must be crazy," I chuckle to myself. "Either that, or I am turning into a dog. It is entirely his fault and I cannot believe the old guy is turning me into a dog," I say, rehearsing the joke in the back of my mind, burying it to dig up for a later performance.

It is here that we come upon the house restored by the couple from Milano. Stone upon stone, cut from stone, pristine, clean, splashes of colour from textile to flower, it is perched in tiers on ledges overlooking the valley below. I am seeing my repatriated dream home. Everything is so near the edge it is frightening. When Vesuvio goes, this house will be the first to slide off the mountain and I will need to walk up again to find my shoes. I declare to Maria that we will come back to live here and I seal the oath with a kiss.

Already in her own enchantment, she takes the kiss and ignores me completely. She is walking arm-in-arm, deep in conversation with her aunt. I behold this nativity, this rebirth and see the lesson immediately. I, *Il Vagabondo*, am witness to the roots of my wife and her family. I see the heritage of my half-Italian children. I am in the birthplace of *Garibaldi's* stories, the treasury of *lezione*, the mother-lode. Everything is in the day and the day is in everything. The Alpha and the Omega of it. I see the libretto and I am a rich man, *Io sono un uomo ricco.*

We are on our way to the *Castillo* now and I walk faster to catch up. Not ten yards from the Milan-house, I am startled by a dog barking. The fence is wire and there are chickens milling about poking their stupid heads right up to the street. There are buckets and shovels, hay and seed strewn about. It is of the housescapes and the terrain of Castropignano and the funny thing is, it all fits together and makes sense.

The *Castillo* has a respectful, weathered look to it. The gate is closed and locked and there is a sign in Italian warning us to stay out. There is no room to walk around the outside because the outside is the edge of the mountain. There is still a tower but it is smaller up close and its fine lines have tumbled into slackness in some places. It has a history I will never really know, like the old guys who play cards at the Club, but you can tell there are stories there and lessons to find, if you want to look for them. To the right, facing east is a small bench that you can sit on to look over the valley. The ledge is steep and only six feet away. There are no fences forcing you to stay back and if you want to fall down the side, you can.

"Once a little girl was playing up here," I tell Nina and Maria. "She tumbled over the edge and went down the side. The women were crying and the bell was ringing. Some men went to get some rope and go down the side to find her."

Maria is smiling and I can tell Nina is looking at me curiously.

"At that time," I continue, "there were no cars like there are today. Some of the people went down the road to the bottom of the hill but it took a long time. When they finally got there, they found the little girl, playing and picking flowers!" I finish with a triumphant flourish.

"You know this?" laughs Nina.

"*Si*. It is because I am smarter than I look, *Signora*," I say.

Maria gently pats my cheek and sighs. Together they walk gracefully over to the castle, arm in arm, completely present in feminine conversation.

I turn and sit on the solitary bench overlooking the valley. My arms are draped over the back. Legs crossed, I am in a peaceful slouch. The light is changing. Suddenly, I am riveted by the fluid scene before me. I sit up. Far across the valley, on the other side, there are a series of hills rising up at bold angles that suggest dimension and a vague feeling of vertigo. The fields of the hills are partitioned off in patches and there are hedgerows bordering some, trees marking others and stone fences sculpting still other spaces. It is too far away to see people. I only see texture and contour, colour and form, moving shadows and shimmering atmosphere. My eye is taken immediately to the frothy orange flames, rolling haphazardly up the side of a field. The smoke curls black in that little corner of sky. Farmers burn off their stubble and you can see the berm ridges of soil herding the flames now this way, now that. I am too distant to smell the scorched trail but I see the black patterned wake and the white, thick smoke roiling off in patches. From that little bench, beside the Castle, next to my wife and her family, I am permitted to see The Divine System, the Grand Garden unfolding before my eyes. It is the Fractal Geometry of Life. They say that by analyzing a foot of a river bank you may determine the entire etched course of the river itself. This landscape lives. I glimpse the lesson, but it moves faster than the flames and flickers out before I fully understand it. But I do understand it because I am in *Garibaldi's* Court. It is as if I see the soul of something, but I can't tell because no one will believe me. It is an eternal tableau of the way life was, the way life is, and the way life is going to be. All told in one animate landscape, yet be quick, the lesson is like a shooting star and you might miss it completely. Or perhaps you will see it out of the corner of your eye or maybe you will be crestfallen that someone else beside you saw it. If you are lucky, one day you will see it head on.

"*Abbi pazienza*," my mother-in-law keeps telling me.

"We are going to see Johnny's Dad!" Maria calls out.

I come to my senses.

We walk up a new road now, one that takes us over another rise and past the long steep steps of the church and the bell tower.

"Once they used this bell to tell time and to announce *importante* things because no one had watches back then," I proudly declare to Nina, so fluent in the libretto.

There is a *piazza* there. Nina points out a window on the second floor and tells us that this is where *Garibaldi* and Lina first had an apartment in town when they were married. It belonged first to *Garibaldi's* older sister and her husband before they went to Argentina.

"It is a government building now," Nina says factually.

I vaguely remember something else about the church but it is like squinting through the surface of water into the depth of memory and I can't see a thing.

We pick our way along a little laneway, then down a flight of steps that open up to a new, slightly broader street. "If you get lost, all you have to do is climb up to the castle and find your bearings from there," I proudly declare. We nod to those passing by and you can tell from their eyes that they know we must be part of Nina's *Americano* family. On the walls are the *Morte* posters announcing in bold black letters who has died and when. I am struck by how matter-of-fact, how public, yet how respectful it is.

"I wonder if they had one of these up for Lina" I ask Maria.

She doesn't know and I make a note to ask Biagio some time but forget to.

Camillo Caperchione's is around the corner from the war monument. To get there, you must pass the open door where the younger girls sell the fine handwork of their mothers. The street hairpins around and overlooks the soccer pitch and beyond that, the new *incarcere*, the prison. There are no prisoners there now, unless you count the kids who had to move from their elementary school building, rendered unsafe by the earthquake. But even this is nothing new. While we head up from the little *piazza* we pass the original school.

"Nina," I say, "did you know this was originally the school in Castropignano *and* the prison? The school was on the second floor and they kept the prisoners along here. Back then, you could only go to grade 5. Some of the more well-to-do families could send their kids the distance to Campobasso, but the rest had to go to work," I finish triumphantly.

"He spends a lot of time with Daddy," Maria says by way of explanation.

"*Ah, si!*" Nina laughs.

We climb the steep steps to Camillo's house. He is father to my friend Johnny from Woodbridge. I get Maria to translate: "Johnny played saxophone and so did his Dad. Back then there was a little orchestra that Angelo tried to organize. There was one musician in the town who knew how to teach. Angelo got some young people together but he never played an instrument himself. Johnny kept playing and now, Nina, you should hear him do "*Come Prima!*" Can you believe, they call him Johnny Sax back home now.

You take your chances climbing the steps in Castropignano. There are no rails and the angle is calibrated for pitons and mountain axes. Inevitably there are four or five cats sunning themselves at the top landing which splits off into laneways leading to other houses. It reminds my knees vaguely of Navajo cliff dwellings. There are drop-offs everywhere and suddenly, I understand why baby fences and socket guards made no sense to the *nonnas* and *nonnos* of North York and why pets are never kept indoors or fed store-bought food.

"No, you don't see that in my country," Angelo says definitively, wincing smugly and waving his hand in an absent circular motion.

We pass through the beaded tentacles into a darkened room while Nina calls out. The beads are hung to let the air in and to keep the flies out. The tentacles cling to our necks and arms and then fall free. Here we are met by Assunta, who cocks her head, listens intently and suddenly understands with a delighted "*Ahh, si, si!*" and an explosive grin of recognition, that this is her cousin Angelo Molinaro's daughter and her *Americano* husband. Camillo sits in a chair to my right. He is very old. His mind leaves gracefully for an interior world where the involuntary movements of his arms and his legs and the beautiful sway of his head won't matter. To me, he is simply beautiful and I get that crazy loyalty feeling again. My eyes well up.

There are kisses and touches and intense listening gazes and we are joined by another of Johnny's sisters, Filomena and her daughter Angela. Camillo looks happy but I can tell he is not quite sure who

Maria is. Assunta explains to him, close to his face, and there is the flare of recognition again. Suddenly, I am asked in Italian if I would like a glass of wine and I accept.

"He is not Italian then?" (I am used to the question …)

(… as well as the inevitable response): "*No, non parlo Italiano*" (translate: furtive glances, nods and hesitant smiles) At this point, and get ready for it, the natural rhythm in the room, the joy, the laughing, the interest completely ignores you!

Lesser men will grow bored, or fidget or complain grumpily afterwards to their wives. But if you want to you can be happy, simply because "you won't die from this." You still have your sight, your sound, your heart, your thoughts, your power of observation, your smile, your laugh. You still possess your love. You are *Il Vagabondo*, the Wanderer, thrown into an ancient story with all of your wits. The *mosto* in the mundane! A bit player, stage left to the Living Opera. The *Canadese* flyer shot down, befriended by an entire hill town and hidden from the Germans. You are just past the light in the *Caravaggio*, curled in the dark, slightly out of view with the pure freedom of invisibility and the heightened sense of wonder that dreams create. It is an enchantment that is induced beyond and without the thickness of homemade red wine.

Happily, I toast Camillo and then the entire room and tell them all that Johnny is my friend and I am honoured to be here. There is a half-hearted translation by Maria who is fully present in the room, within the conversation. You must remember and will be told, during and later, that the privilege of invisibility is a toll on the double duty of the translator.

The phone rings. Assunta gets up to answer it. There is the sound of animated conversation. She re-enters the room and announces with disbelief that it is none other than Johnny on the phone, calling from Woodbridge. He does not even know that Maria and I are here. Everyone talks to him and the excitement level is raised a notch. Maria speaks to him, then Assunta and then someone is gesturing for me to come over to the telephone. Johnny wants to talk to me.

My English pours out like water from a fifty-gallon drum.

"Johnny we are here! Here in your Dad's house! It is so beautiful! Yes, he is fine. He looks good. Johnny I am drinking your Dad's wine in the house you grew up in. It couldn't be better. Are you playing a wedding tonight?" And after a while: "*Assunta, parle Johnny per favore,*" I say grandly.

There is more laughter, sight, sound and wine. Johnny has pushed me into *Caravaggio's* light. Later, at the next wedding, I will tell him the story and our wide arms will measure our amazement.

I can see by the shadows in the room that the sun is on the move. There are kisses and touch as one by one, we part the beaded curtain, step over the cats and sidestep our way down the stairs. Everyone has come out on the landing to say goodbye. The cedars stand out first and then the warm yellow fields and the vivid green of the woods beyond, stretching in the shade. We head up and around. The doorway to the lace booth is closed up. There is activity over by the large *piazza*, a barbecue is going and people start to collect and mill about. We climb up to the main street past the old school building, the shop where you can buy meat, the government office on the right and up ahead, the small *piazza* where men are playing cards. The restaurant where we buy *gelato* and *benezene*, off to the left, yawns open its metal awning to announce the robust evening. Our children pass, going the other way in a gaggle of cousins and friends. They stand out like *Americanos* but look like they are content.

Nina calls something out to Kristina that I don't understand but I somehow know she has said to meet us later at *Zio* Domenico's.

There is no rush. We don't have to be anywhere at exactly 8 or no later than 9. We arrive when we arrive (*shrug shoulders here*), sometime in the evening.

I am not sure which angle we ascend but I think it is in the direction of the church. A stairway takes us down to a road, we walk along that and get over close to the walls when the cars pass by. There is a break in the stone and we head down another broken flight of stairs out to the paved road that leads to *Zio* Domenico's. In the left corner of my eye, I recognize the prison and get that pleased feeling of knowing exactly where I am. I cross check that with a sighting of the Castle, now seen from another angle and Eureka! The disorientation has passed. I know how to get back home. And all of a sudden, it feels like home. I have broken in my new suit of clothes. They are no longer stiff. They ride comfortably on me now and I find myself flopping on the bed and leaving my toothbrush in the bathroom, my laundry bag on the floor. Castropignano claims me for its own. I am no longer a tourist.

[Act II]

Scene 2.

Serenade. An Evening at Domenico's

The Inglese gets to know the old guy's brother

Everyone is now at Domenico's. Biagio and Enzo are intent around the barbecue. Gabriele is crying and Noemi is tired and squabbling. Enrica looks intense and Marica serene. *Zia* Maria and Nina move to and fro, getting the table ready. Salvatore turns his laptop computer into a karaoke and the older children sing lyrics. I see a thin-looking dog and a couple of new cats. Our children look tired and a little disconnected. I invite Adriana to play a clapping game called Hi Lo Chikolo. Together: open and closed hand, open and closed hand, open and closed hand, *clap, clap, clap.* Like a dinner bell, the children drift over to watch. Open and closed hand, open and closed hand, open and closed hand, *clap, clap, clap.* Soon everyone is having a go at it. Gabriele has stopped crying and even little Noemi has overcome her shyness to try Hi Lo Chikolo with the *Americano.* They are all in the happy trance of play. Maria gravitates to the kitchen and I make my way up, past the cement patio and stone wall, to the garage. A couple of hens waddle by and a rooster is on the road. The barbecue smells exquisite. Upon enquiry I am told that Domenico has killed one of his chickens and among many other things, this is what we will eat. He is younger than *Garibaldi* but his white hair makes him look older. We have met, once before. It was about twenty years ago when he and *Zia* Maria came to Toronto and to Welland to see her family.

Even when he is talking in Italian I can tell he speaks even less than Angelo. He gestures with his hands and makes a "choo" sound a lot when he changes thoughts. His face is crinkled around the eyes and he has the slow-moving look of a man who works hard, speaks little, and sees all. His eyes twinkle when he is amused and I can tell he has already observed me and formed some sort of opinion.

"You look like your brother," I say to him in a sort of pidgin English, blended with Italian nouns and plenty of hand gestures. I think he understands. He tends the fire and I work hard at thinking about how to engage him.

"*La terra e molto bene*," I say making a sweeping gesture with my hands. "*La casa e bella!*" Little does he know that I am saying: "Your house and your land are so beautiful. I am honoured to be here and I can't believe how wonderful everything is. Your brother is one of my best friends and because of that I am going to get to know you whether you like it or not. Your wife Maria has the same laughing eyes as Lina and for this reason alone, I really like her and I want to be her friend."

There is a pause and all that emotion is packed into two desperate universal phrases:

"*Do-men-i-co*," I say with mock drama. "Do-you-play *scopa*?" I gesture dealing cards with my hands. "Do you—*come si dice?*—do you make wine? I make it with Angelo," I add, pantomiming a turning, crushing gesture with my bare hands stretched along the cold steel bar of an imaginary press.

He says something I don't understand, tries again and then gestures for me to follow him.

We pass by the triumphant karaoke singers on the cement patio.

"*Ciao*, Salvatore!" I say.

"*Buonasera*," he says smiling, along with something else I hope means "How are you?"

"*Bene grazie*," I say in mild panic.

We pass by the long table at the end of the house. It is perfectly shaded by two well placed apple trees and bordered by a little stone wall. Perched proudly overlooking the back, this table waits quietly, poised to announce the view. I stoop underneath a limb and pick my way along a little stone path. A thin cat winces, hesitates and then darts back up the small hill. This is "Moosh-Moosh" we are told, favoured among the pride. (Later we learn that all of the cats are called Moosh-Moosh.) Standing straight, I am able to look up now and take in the Italian-scape stretching out before me. My sight is fluid and my spirit walks right into the oily contours and earthen smells of living art. First I see a reddish orange sun reflecting off the fields, leading me to the quiet cool-white walls of the cemetery, a half mile away and to the left. It is bordered intermittently by tall, thin cedars peacefully standing vigil. Beyond that is the green roll of the woods swelling out indefinitely.

Domenico points and I follow his sight line way out to a little house completely overgrown. This is the Tullo-house and beyond that, one of the "pieces of land" that they once walked out to.

"Back then, if you wanted to get someplace, there were no cars or even roads like there are now. No, you had to walk everywhere," *Garibaldi* tells me when I sit with him alone around the kitchen table in his house on Rita Drive. He built the kitchen with his bare hands and with his own son: drywall, plumbing, gas line, wiring. A *paesano* came in to do the ceramic tile and twenty years later, it still looks like the grouting was just done.

"It is the *Ceramica Bella* that makes the kitchen look so good," I tease him and while he is taking the bait, I quietly shake my head at the way guys do work now. Cutting corners, fudging it, making things fit as opposed to refitting. Once the paint dries and they are all gone, you see more of what they didn't do and what they did do is barely adequate.

"There is very little pride now," I tell him. "It is all about the money." And surprisingly he concedes the point.

Garibaldi is always at the end, at the head of the table, in front of the little 50s-style sliding glass dining hutch. It holds the wine glasses, the *espresso* cups, the electric percolator and the strong dark mixture of coffee and *Barzula* espresso beside the box of paper filters. Behind the sliding wooden doors, tucked away underneath is the alcohol: rye, Sambucca, vermouth, always full and used rarely except to toast on Christmas Eve and other holiday occasions. And then there is the array of little miniature bottles suggesting trips somewhere long ago and more stories. Over his left shoulder, next to the crucifix, he will erect a jerry-built shrine to his departed wife, with pictures of family descending in proximity to his heart. Curiously, he will move his spot to sit, always, where she sat and where he alone can see the shrine. And I realize now that I moved my chair to face him that once, in the living equinox, I used to sit at the opposite end. So my place is newly on the left, in the middle, facing the door underneath the stairs. But always, there is the little gas stove with its steaming, boiling pot of water, the gurgling spattering pot of sauce, the kitchen counter, cabinets and the fridge covered with garish magnets of hens pecking roosters, plastic picture frames, *Jesu* and a guardian angel airily watching over two little children. Over my head is the plate from Bermuda that we brought back for them from our honeymoon. Inevitably, the dishes are efficiently done by Maria and Lina who then go outside to the front to sit and to pass time. The children are in the basement watching TV. It is after the meal and after the work is done. I have gone already to the *cantina* to refill the bottle of wine because it is that time when old men talk to young men, if they will listen.

"We had nothing," he continues in a tone that causes me to pay more attention. He holds me in his full gaze now, looks me straight in the eye and I can tell he wants me to understand. "We had nothing but we were happier than we are today!" he says rapping the table for effect, sitting back triumphantly.

"We would get up in the dark and have a little piece of bread, if we were lucky," he says. He always makes a sawing motion with an imaginary knife across his three fingers as if they are a loaf of bread. "Then we would walk for miles and go to work in the fields ... whatever there was to do, pick-the-corn, gather-the-wheat, dig-the-field ... we didn't have tractors like they do today."

Sometimes I tell him a story back. It is my way of showing respect, of connecting with the *signore*, for while I may be the Italian Night School Drop-out I am showing up for the stories and learning to speak them fluently.

"Yes, and do you remember?" I interject, "that time Lina and Ermelinda walked way out to bring you food? It was late morning, probably around a quarter to eleven and when the women showed up it was time to take the break. One time, Linda was walking over these ridges and she fell down. The container of pasta fell off her head and it all spilled into the dirt. They were so afraid, so you know what they did? They gathered it up and brushed it off as best they could. They brought it out to you and to the other men as if there were nothing wrong. You all started to eat it and it tasted gritty." I make a face and pretend I am spitting out dirt.

Garibaldi finishes his laugh and the echo is still merry in his eyes.

"Yes. I remember," he says looking at me differently.

Encouraged by this, sometimes, when I feel like teasing him, I will take the story right over.

"I don't know if you did this," I say in my instructive tone, "but they didn't use the water back then to clean the dishes. What they used to do was grab the plates and rub dirt around them like this and that made them clean. The women gathered them up, took them home, did more work and then they came back out later with more food.

"At least, that's the way it used to be," I finish with a flourish.

And then, as if I am turning the next page I say, "Sometimes it was so far to walk out to the piece of land and so late when they finished, that they would take some of the stalks of the corn, bundle them together to make a sort of tent or—how do you say it?—like a teepee and then they would sleep in the fields, get up before the sun and start working again the next day."

"That's right," he says, enjoying *his* tale.

"That was our life," I say shrugging my shoulders to make the point. "You will not remember this," I say baiting the hook even more, "but they used to bring the ears of corn all the way back and dump them in huge piles in Gino's front yard. People from the neighbouring farm would come over and after a long day in the field, everyone would sit around in a circle and husk *the* corn. There was singing and dancing and good food. It was—how do I say it in your language?—your *re-cre-ati-oni*," I conclude, casually gesturing with the forefingers and thumb of my left hand pursed together.

By this time, it is getting late and we are full with conversation. Content. We top up our glasses from what is left in the bottle of wine. We drain it in one go and amble outside to the front to pass time with the girls. Inevitably, one of the women from the street stops by and we are greeted with the music of "*Ciao* Angelo!" accompanied by a big smile and a "Hello" in English, for me.

"*Buonasera, Signora*," I say and select a lawn chair where I can put my feet up. It is one of the privileges of being ignored and besides, it is not unusual for *Il Vagabondo* to be forced into sleep by the narcotic of the wine cut with the *gassosa* of fresh air.

But now, Domenico's new gesture pulls my gaze to the foreground. "Choo!"

My eyes slowly walk in from the Tullo land and the tree line. I see now the *giardino autentico*, the authentic garden in a free-spirited backyard that could run out to the cemetery and beyond. There is a new lesson here, but it is subtle and slightly out of view. *Garibaldi's* garden back home is a work of art. Every square inch seems to have a purpose or to be connected in sequence, to a purpose. His sister Enedina's garden has a woman's beauty, logic and thoughtfulness grafted to its system. *Zio* Giovanni's has a different personality altogether. His tomatoes are from the lost planet, over six feet tall, and he plants peppers around the trees in the front. He sank his own makeshift well into the ground to keep the water cool. He uses the bottom part of one of his plastic fifty-gallon drums and covers it with a round piece of plywood with a rope handle.

"The wine was better back in Italy," *Garibaldi* says to me. "It was more, ahh, I can't think of the word now, it was more … natural. We didn't use the chemicals like they use today to keep them from ripening too soon. Everything was natural," he repeats.

"What are you talking about?" I say. "You have changed my palate forever," I add referring to the wine at the old place at 23 Rita. "I, *Il Vagabondo,* can no longer drink store-bought wine and it is your fault! Yours is fuller. It is stronger and the taste is—*come si dice?*—primitive. Giovanni's is good, *Zio* Carmine's is excellent but ours is the best!" I declare, rapping the table for a little punctuation.

Yet here with Domenico, in Castropignano, I see that the gardens back home, while beautiful, are like little restrained replicas, like a spirit-in-a-box, like a horse in a stall, like a house cat devoid of its Serengeti roots; maybe even a little like an immigrant, magnificent despite the imposed restrictions of lot and an owned little piece of land that cannot really sing the old songs no matter how hard you till it. You lose these things forever when you go but your spirit will still produce, you will still make a life, you will come from nothing and make something that puts every *Inglese* garden in need of that much more water. But it is different back home. I can see it now.

Domenico's garden is wild. There are no fences. The soil is reddish brown and crusty. It looks dry and crumbles like cake with an interior moistness. The rows are longer, wider and there are more of them. The tomatoes you see first. The zucchini, the eggplant … all the usual stuff and then you see the vines, hooked up to poles and connected along the entire row.

"Wow," I say in English and then add, "*la molto bella terra!*" I point to the hoses.

We make contact and he proudly explains his watering system by walking me through the entire process. There are a series of small hoses, running from the central source, elevated on little tripods spanning the whole garden. This is his so-called Grade 5 engineering design for getting the water from the house all the way to any spot in the garden.

"Your brother has to see this," I say and I think he gets it.

"Together, Domenico, you and I must force Angelo to come over," I say, feeling braver, somehow pantomiming the whole thing by pointing, twisting my arm and flying an Alitalia plane across an imaginary ocean with the palm of my hand.

We laugh. We are starting to *comprendi*.

He takes me now to his *cantina*. He is letting me get to know him. I realize he is talking to me the way *Garibaldi* talks to me—not with the words but by walking, pointing, showing, tasting, gesturing, watching, demonstrating, passing things for me to touch. It is a much fuller expression but you will miss it completely if you do not see the libretto in *Garibaldi's* Court. You could grow impatient. You could excuse yourself and look to be rescued from the deafening silence by your wife. Later you could get angry with her, know you are wrong, but argue anyway.

"It is impossible to get through to those old Italian guys," you could tell your Canadian friends later on in a pub. They will nod their heads. There are a thousand ways to avoid getting to know the strange, the unique and the different.

Later, at 10:30 at night, with Maria's help, we will stand with *Zia Nina e Zia* Maria in an open-air kitchen converted from the stall where the pigs and the sheep and Rosie are kept. I will tell them a story of *Gusto*. It can only be told under the stars when you take a break from the gas stove, from *Polenta la scuola*, nibbling cheese and sipping wine.

"When we were first going out, she would come over to see me and I would try to feed her Heinz spaghetti sauce in a can," I say incredulously.

"She would refuse and get mad at me and threaten to throw the pots all over the room," I say pausing for dramatic effect and a gesture of sympathy from the older women.

"How will we fall in love?" I say. "What am I going to do? But then she took me to Lina's for the first time for pasta. My first red boiling smells, celery and bowls of green and black olives. I don't think I knew black olives existed until then, let alone knew they came out of a can. Warm, shivery sips of *la tassa*. My first spare ribs sliding off the bone, hard pieces of sausage, shredded cubes of veal clinging along the ridges of steaming *penne rigate*. Airy, chewy bread to soak it all up, oil and vinegar salad with lots and lots of glorious salt biting the inside of your mouth, thick, red wine to gulp it down, with "S" biscuits, fruit and *espresso* for after.

"Maria. Nina. It was everything—how do I say it?—an Enchantment!

"That is how I got so fat," I say sadly. "But I am in love and I know what *gusto* means," I triumphantly conclude while making my mouth corners go down like *Il Duce*.

"*Bravo, Vagabondo!*" they cry.

I bend my neck and shrug my shoulders. "Choo."

Now the *cantina* is not necessarily a guy place but I feel very comfortable there. It seems to span half the underside of Domenico's house. On the outside there is a smooth sort of a foundational wall but on the inside, the dimensional length looks like it is cut right into the stone. There are ledges and recesses and a little dark anteroom. Ali Baba and his forty thieves would be at home here. I see green demijohns of red wine gleaming, and odd-shaped gallons and always a slightly larger container of experimental white wine fermented as an afterthought. Sausages hang, a proscuitto I think, and the air smells musty and damp. I find myself wanting to eat again, or to at least sample one of everything in the jars on the wooden shelf. Domenico is my guide now and he points to these bottles and I realize he is offering me a *benezene*. A *birra*. Always, there is an opener in a *cantina*, usually screwed into a good thick two-by-six inch plank but if it is not anchored down there will be one or two on a chain in an oily wooden box. It is all part of the spinning systems-within-systems forged through the trial and error of experiences that make life efficient: simpler, running smoothly.

Clink! We toast. I see him smiling and I know he has formed another opinion of his brother's son-in-law.

Using all the nouns I can muster, all the gestures and growing more comfortable just plain talking clumsy English, I take a good run at telling him the *cantina* story about the boy who stole the sausages.

"When we were little kids we were hungry and could never get anything to eat," Angelo begins with a chuckle. "We used to keep our sausages in a clay pot, like an urn, and fill it up with grease from the pig. It would grow hard and white and that is how we kept them from going bad. There was one guy that tipped over the pot and made a little hole in the bottom. From that hole, he would sneak into the *cantina* and dig out a little piece of sausage. He used to sneak in all the time, take a little piece and stand the pot back up. One day the father went into the *cantina* to get some sausages. He pushed down and broke through the top and found the pot was empty. Oh, did the boy get some trouble!"

It is hard to know if Domenico understands the story or not but somehow it doesn't matter. He is carrying a large faceted bottle of red wine now. I follow him out of the dark *cantina* and we step out into the light. My eyes adjust. I trail behind him along the back of the house. He shows me the little kitchen and the gas stove and beside that, near the end of the house where the outdoor patio table waits, I see a large wooden door. He opens it and we have to step up over the threshold. We enter the stone, cave-like chamber. The family's original wine press stands majestically before us. It is the wine press of *Garibaldi's* grandfather: *il torchio di nonno*. It is huge and made entirely of wood, including the cogs for cranking the press. I know I am seeing a monument of the past. I am made to understand that it is still working. I touch it and take its picture as if it is a living thing.

"*Dio! Magnifico!*" is all I can say to Domenico.

He smiles and nods and we step outside and walk up the stone steps to the table. There is dinner and later, more food at *Polenta* School, laughter, squawks, whines and singing. Enzo lights a cigarette and the smoke hangs in the air, then catches a breeze and slips off into the night. When it is somehow time, we hug, there are kisses, *ciaos* and promises to see each other tomorrow.

Maria and I, the children in tow, pick our way up the worn steps to the street, over and up the next stone flight that leads to the *piazza* and around the bend to Biagio's and home. I am a rich man, and that much more in love.

Scene 3.

The Cemetery and the Fig Pastoral

An importante passeggiata, lezioni *abound*

The next day comes. I take out our laundry and hang it on the line. It is already hot and bright. The natural white from the stone makes me squint and I look up into the solid blue of the sky to clear my vision. Somehow, our day is already arranged. The sheep will be led. It is a wonderful feeling.

"*Ciao*, Nina," I call out to the other step. "*Buongiorno*," I say. "*La bella giornata*."

"*Buongiorno*," she sings back. And then she says something else that I later find out from Maria means, Did you sleep well?

"*Dormi, dormi, dormi*," I say to myself over and over, trying to bake it permanently into the oven of my mind. It blows a fuse every time I have to actually converse with someone.

"*Si, grazie*," I call back cleverly.

Nina is off somewhere and leaves behind a feeling of anticipation that heralds in a knowledge that something new will happen today.

Soon my family is ready and we step out into a blast of bright white blue from the tiny courtyard. I turn, fiddle with the lock and get it right. Through the little laneway and just to the left on the street below the *piazza*, we part new, beaded curtains and Maria calls out to her *Zia*. The kitchen is always the first space to greet us. We are pulled inside with hugs and sound and kisses. There is Cousin Nicola. He is in his 60s, walks with a swagger and has a Clark Gable-style moustache.

I like him immediately. We meet his wife Maria, and then we are all presented to old *Zia* Maria.

She is stooped and beyond beautiful. Her eyes well up, (*my*) Maria's eyes well up, and they hold each other, grasping both arms, slightly apart the way women do to look deeply into one another's spirit. They stroke each other's arms and cheeks and beam and nod and say things. The next thing I know they are together on the couch, still holding one another, not really talking. It is one of my favourite things about my Italian family, this simply being present with one another. Talk if you want to or don't talk. Look at each other and smile. Let silence remember and evoke. Sit together. Quietly live. The kids seem to understand this strange sphere and it must enchant them in an unknown way because they don't complain. They are content to be led wherever we go. I think of *Garibaldi* and somehow I understand the unspoken lesson. Parents as shepherds on the stage of the Divine System. Innately, they know this is Mom's time and their Dad looks like he is having fun. In less than a minute, they happily drink orange pop and reluctantly accept strange-looking cookies from faraway lands.

Slowly, when it is time—there is no rush—we learn that Nicola is going to show us around.

The expedition takes us up, around the corner to the *piazza*, up the same narrow street past the monument and the hairpin turn to Camillo's. We see a new part of town and pass the *pizzeria* where we will dine another day with Biagio's family. I will have my first *pizza margherita*. The green is the basil, the white is the cheese and the red is the sauce. The Italian Flag of my stomach and one of the best pizzas I will ever eat.

Nicola gestures that we should go in and before I know it we stand at the little bar, sipping a *benezene* which roughly translates as "gas" but is actually drunk as Nastro Azzuro beer, the Blue Ribbon.

"You and I must play *scopa* in the *piazza*," I say, gesturing the deal.

He smiles and I know he understands my meaning. Poorly spoken nouns, sign language, and gestures are dressed up as emerging friendship.

It is time to go. We are outside, on the move, winding our way slowly up to La Palma: the pretender to the throne of Castropignano, now that the *Castillo* is closed. A modern resort, hotel, conference centre, swimming pool, dance hall all-in-glorious-one. It stands pinkly on the edge of town, its hands on its hips, beckoning every one up from the piazza by the monument, the *bocci* courts, the soccer pitch and other old fashioned places that need no preservative.

It is like that here. All in one place you see flames burning up the side of a hill, a fourteenth-century stone castle crumbling on one side of town, a prison, a cemetery, a school, farmed land, a modern house from *Milano* next to a yard of chickens, a bar with a roll-up awning overlooking cobbled stones and an entertainment aerie perched on a hill within walking distance (translate: "up") of everything. And in the evening, when you are ready, there is *pizza margherita* to eat in or to go. Everything seems to blend together. You make do with what you have. No wonder the first and second wave of Italians adapted to North York. Come to think of it, no wonder an English guy can make a life in *Garibaldi's* Court.

Nicola has a word with the proprietor. He looks proud. He takes a key and gets permission to go up to the roof of La Palma. We overlook the town. I see all the landmarks from here and cross-check my bearings.

We climb down and in a moment we sip another *benezene.*

Hands gratefully shaken, we head out of La Palma up to a little piece of land that Nicola works. He rises each morning at five and walks up to his "garden". We see a thin dog and a little one-room hut. The soil has that same wild, crumbly look, moist on the inside. Together we inspect his garden system. His Maria is already there. We sit and eat fresh bread and cheese, in the little shed planted between fruit trees and vines, rows of tomatoes and zucchini, *fagioli* and cabbage. Little lizards scurry about. The land, the couple, the *Americanos,* the dog, the sky, the air ... everything is content.

Maria and Nicola talk. When it is time I learn that we will head to the cemetery. Later, when it is again time—there is no rush—we will drive up to the family home, *la casa Mascitelli,* on my wife's mother's side. We are invited to dinner at *Zia* Ermelinda's sometime in the evening.

The road leading to the cemetery is over by Domenico's place. It ends, straight as a plank, about a half-mile past the prison. Nicola leads us up the stoney side path to the black wrought-iron gate. He pushes up the latch and walks in with the deliberate step of somebody who has been here before. He takes us directly to the grave site of Maria's maternal grandparents. As we walk, I gaze at the names on the ground and on the walls. They read like the names from our wedding invitation list: Sergnese, Tullo, Meffe, Mascitelli, Molinaro, Iocca, Venditti. My mind is swept back to our wedding reception line at Rizzo's on Albion Road. The dark cognac is for the men, the light cognac is for the women, the little swan *bomboniera* stacked at the end and the hard white candy, symbolizing fertility, wrapped in netting. I see a procession of small, beautiful people making their way towards us. The men are in their dark suits, the women are in their new dresses of green and blue, lilac and pink. The glint of gold jewelry. From the sideline I see each of them steal a furtive glance at Angelo to see if he is happy. Word has gotten out. His daughter is marrying a *Canadese* who does not speak *Italiano* and is a non-*Catolico*. But Angelo *is* happy and because of that, my face is pulled down and I gaze again and again into old, wrinkled, smiling faces that kiss me on both cheeks.

"*Grazie Signore e Signora*," I say, quietly. "*Prego.*"

Later I am at the bar with my brother, amidst the music, the merriment, and the dancing. He comments on the same enchantment. He is loved too. It is the way things are with them.

A gentle breeze brings me back to the grave site and I have my arms around Maria. She pushes things around in her purse. Carefully, she pulls out a roll of tape, a dried palm frond and a copy of a picture. It is a copy of the one on the front of the granite slab of Lina's *appartamento* at the Holy Supper Mausoleum back home. Gently, we secure our gifts, say the Italian prayer and stand back with a sigh knowing that our pilgrimage is complete. Lina has come back to Castropignano to be with her parents. She returns with her daughter to holy ground.

Nicola waits patiently for us. When he thinks we are ready, he says something to Maria. He walks us to the gravesite of Maria's paternal *nonni*. We move down a cobbled pathway and suddenly we are shocked to see a picture we recognize. It is the daughter of my friends

Johnny and Marianina Caperchione. Rita died too young. She is so lovely. Someone has taped her picture to her grandparent's grave. We stand sadly. We pray for Rita, for Johnny and Marianina, for her brother Camillo, for her husband and her three children. They are *Garibaldi's* people and because I am in his Court, they become my family, each of them, all of them. I look over my shoulder to ensure that the children see everything. It is the *prima lezione* and I am pleased that they stand witness to it.

"*La Famiglia* is everything," I say seriously to Nicola and he nods.

At the paternal grandparents' grave site, we touch the name and uneasily take a picture so we can show it to *Garibaldi*. I notice that the children reflexively stand in the shade. "To learn, you have to experience the thing," the old guy always says and I realize, with a chuckle, it is another lesson and a sign that we are no longer tourists. We inherently stop standing in the sun and learn to seek out the cool shade when standing still.

Half-heartedly now, we follow Nicola through a maze of narrow walkways to find ourselves descending down stone steps into a little crypt. We sidestep cobwebs and fight to exhale the damp, urinous smells. Maria whispers to me that these are her great grandparents and I turn to tell the children. The English words echo off the walls. They call eerily out of place above us, around and below. It is remarkably cool underground but we are glad to pick our way back up the steps and into the fresh air.

It is time to go. Nicola leads us back out to the wrought iron gate. I lift the latch, pull it aside and close it with a sharp *clang* when everyone exits. We are back on the road that leads past the prison, walking slowly, vaguely shaking off wisps of memory that still cling to us.

Soon we appear along the stone steps, across the little street from Nicola's house. *Zia* Maria is out to meet us. She wears a head scarf like a towel draped across her head. Her dress is black and she carefully picks her way across the cobbles with her cane. We go across the way to the moist, translucent shade of Nicola's little garden while a breeze gently flutters sunlight through large grape leaves.

"*E Magnifico!*" I say to Nicola, bending down to enter the beautiful space. My eyes focus on tightly packed clusters of grapes weighted sensually throughout the green canopy.

"These are called '*kiki*'," I say out loud, to Nicola and he nods.

I know a little bit about the vines and a little bit about the grapes because I have attended *Garibaldi's* Wine School many times. The *kiki* are the tightly packed clusters of grapes, bunched together without spaces. It is a sign that it is a good year for the grapes when they grow tightly together and are evenly sized. You buy them this way back home at Valencia, at Jane and Sheppard.

Nicola proudly gestures for us to follow him into the middle of his garden.

"Maria," I say urgently, "how do you say 'oasis' in Italian?" " 'Oasis'," I repeat. "How do you say it?"

But Maria is ignoring me. She is tired of translating and finds *Zia* Maria's arm. Together they sit on a little stone bench, holding hands, talking quietly and touching. A lesser man would be offended by such a rebuttal but *Il Vagabondo* has learned the lesson.

In the early days in *Garibaldi's* Court it is not unusual to sit in the kitchen with any number of Italians who laugh, talk all at once and punctuate their joy with bangs on the table. It is so loud and happy. At some point, you ask for a translation. It is not unusual for them to look at you, surprised that you are even there in the first place, skip a beat and then go on laughing, talking and arguing. It is as if the entire conversation bunches up arm-in-arm and walks away from you, with barely a look over its shoulder. Yes, some men would complain but others know that it is the way it is and frankly, like I say, you won't die from this.

"*Ahh, abbi pazienza,*" I say to Maria with a practiced scowl. I make an up-and-down chopping gesture in her direction, with my left hand. You are not the boss of me. I can speak the life!

"Nicola," I say, "It is like a—*come si dice?*—oh-ay-sis in here!"

He cocks his head slightly and replies with what seems like thirty minutes' worth of Italian. I see now what he wants to show me.

"*Uno vigne,*" he says proudly. His index finger points at me to punctuate the claim.

"*Uno vigne,*" he repeats, cupping both hands to show width.

"*E incredibile!*" I say in reply. And it really is incredible. The entire breadth of Nicola's vineyard is spanned by the branches and tendrils of this one robust vine. It is an extraordinary plant singing its bright green song between the white and grey stone buildings. I feel proud just looking at it.

The children and I inspect the strong pale undersides of leaves and touch clusters of grapes. There is motion and I see it is time to go next door for some *panini* and cheese, bread and melon, wine and more orange pop. It is so good to sit. It is a *bella giornata* and I am beyond *contento*, so alive in *paradiso*.

After a time, a car pulls up. We pile inside. I am made to understand that we will drive up to the house that is the birthplace of Maria's mother. The road curves and curves again. The houses herd smaller together and before I know it, I am in the expanse of fields. My bearings are completely gone. All I know is that the Castle is back that way because I can make it out in the distance when the road veers around. We stop. Another car pulls up behind us. Expectantly, we see who pours out. It is *Zia* Ermelinda, Maria's other newly rediscovered aunt. She is driven by Nicola's nephew, Angelo, who together with his wife, Concetta, and their little daughter, Raffaella, will be our new hosts of the evening.

Maria goes to the front passenger side to help Ermelinda out. Another beauty dressed in black emerges. She is shaking and squints into Maria's face like it is the sun. We rub long-lost tears and make way for hugs, embraces and touch. The children and I are presented to Angelo.

"*Buonasera*," I say shaking his hand. "*Piacere*," a pleasure.

Furtive talking ensues, nodding, and I know I am being discussed in the third person.

The children are now touched and pinched and kissed, hugged and laughed at for being so tall. For the hundredth time I hear how much they look like Maria. I make a joke to myself that at least they don't have my chopped-liver genes. Chuckling, it is so easy to side-step the un-enchanted thought.

"*Buonasera, Signora*," I say, grinning. I am pulled down now to cheek level and my eyes are looked into, deeply. It happens quickly but the sensation is one of having my interior, my character walked through, inspected and left. All in a moment and it is not unpleasant. I do a little gazing myself. The Court of *Garibaldi* has that effect. When you are not talking there is more time to observe, to listen, to hear, to scrutinize and to perceive.

When I am pulled down this close to a face I cannot miss the eyes and if I do I am a fool. Her eyes are just like Lina's. Come to think of it, so are *Zia* Maria's and the other *Zia* Maria, Domenico's wife. Later I will have a chance to see Concetta's eyes and my curiosity will be satisfied. The eyes are very fluid. Around the corners you see a little anxiety, a little worry. This is quickly offset by the wrinkles in the outer corners which grin in repose and then multiply happily when pushed by a smile. The actual eyes, green, brown, blue, all appear to be black, perfectly round and slightly moist. Sometimes the dark gleam within gives them even more dimension. It is a sensation of looking apprehensively over the edge and down into the well. When my own eyes adjust, I see past the circumference. There is no boundary other than a deep pool that reflects enough light to suggest depth. Once I see this I am too close and I must step back to focus and get a more expansive view. If I keep looking into the moist blackness I see many things. I will never be completely sure of what I see, but I will see, and what I do see is how much they love, how much they forgive and walk around the foibles of their men, how hard life has been, how utterly tired they are, how much they know about the way of life that they are not saying, the day after day of endless giving, stirring around like a spoon in steaming pasta, or the circles of olive oil on salad. These eyes are the secret communion of knowing that women have with other women.

"It is like flames going up the side of a field," I catch myself thinking.

Now we see the house. It is behind a tall hedge of bramble trying to be trees yet not really making it. The grass is long and it could be an old face we gaze into.

"I've heard stories about this place," I say, slowly to Nicola. He is moving around to the side. He disappears around the back, intent on seeing something. The door is intact but a half-glance through the window tells me that no one has been inside for years. We are taken to the side. Maria is up ahead and I see Ermelinda point her cane up to the second floor.

Maria turns to me happy.

"That is Mamma's room," she says. "We have to get a picture!"

"This is where *Zia* Linda stayed when *Zio* Giovanni came over to Canada. Filomena was here, too!"

"Wow," I say in awe. It is one thing to hear about a place but to stand beside it evokes a sacred feeling.

"That's *Nonna's* room," I tell the kids, completing the chain of command, "right over there by that little door is where Mamma's *Zia* Linda stayed."

Carefully, we pick our way along the overgrown side to the back. Old vines beg at our cuffs imploring us not to rush. The land rolls down steeply towards the left and there are fields swelling below that and to the right. I see a stand of what looks like bamboo and take the kids over to inspect it.

"*Come si chiama*, Angelo?" I ask.

I am made to understand that it is called "*Cane*" (*kah-nay*).

"*Ahhh, si, grazie*," I say.

My mind flows back to the sad time when I work hard to distract *Garibaldi*. We are at the table. It is evening. I remove a stack of veal from the downstairs refrigerator and pry the pieces apart. Guilia, his neighbour, left them. They lay like salt cod in rigor mortis, flash-frozen and stacked inside plastic bags. I finish frying up a pair of veal in a tiny bit of oil. They cook quickly. I pat them dry and we serve them plain, with bread and spicy Molisano sausages preserved in oil. The long uncut sausages are unbelievably hard to fish out of the jar, they are wedged together so tightly. There is a technique to putting *onetwo* tines of a fork into the end to shimmy out the first one, halfway. Remove it with your fingers and then the rest will follow easily. If you get the oil on your shirt there will be trouble. There is a half-eaten dish of green beans sitting in the fridge so I pull that out too.

"She left me," he says, grief-stricken, shaking his head.

"*Si*," I say quietly.

We eat alone in silence for a time. Our eyes dry.

"Angelo," I say, "you are slipping. How come you didn't tell me about the bamboo guards you place over your fingers so the scythe doesn't cut them off? We call them *cannello*. I am not sure what you call them or if you even used them but if you pay attention I will give you the *lezione*."

I have his attention now and the shadows slip from his face. He looks at me.

"You see. You go like this. You slip the cones over the fingers of your left hand. You grab the—how do you say it?—the grain, like this. You take the scythe and make the cut. *Perfetto*! Are you listening? The young must always make the time to teach the old!"

He grins now. He is coming back from the sad place.

"Did you know," I say triumphantly, "that we used to put sheepskin over our arms to protect our skin from the barbs of the wheat?"

"Ahh, you think you know, but you don't know," he tells me with a dismissive flourish of his left hand.

"We had those," he says, now fully present. "We used them for grain and for shearing the sheeps too."

"Maria-at-work showed them to me when I was telling her about our steamer trunk idea," I tell him. "I am surprised you didn't tell me about this. You remind me of what my father used to say to me: 'I taught you everything I know and still you know nothing!' I will have to tell Maria about the sheep. You see, the only way you learn is when I listen!" I say, triumphantly.

He grabs my hands and pretends to grip them hard.

"*Eeeh, ehhh, ehhh, ehhh*," he winces and smiles, standing.

I clear the dishes and then we go outside to pass some time.

The children and I rub our hands along the bamboo, feeling its hardness, its shiny texture, the ridges at each joint. I tell them how *Nonno* used to protect his fingers during harvest and they nod. There is an old thresher in the back, unspooled in sharp, rusty circles. Time has turned it into a sculpture as opposed to a thing of use.

I look off in the distance and see the river far below. The moment is expansive and I want to call Nicola to tell him about the *mangina* ("*Eh, don't ask me how to spell it!*") and the *Telio* (*tell-eye-oh*) machines. In the old days they used to cut a particular reed with a hard stalk on the outside covering a fibrous core. They take the reeds down to the river in bundles and set them under the water. You must put a rock on them so they aren't swept away by the current. After about *twothree* days you pull them out and take them back to the house. There is a machine they built like a sawhorse. One side comes up like one of those paper cutters you see in schools. You place the reeds over the edge and bring the handle side down in a sort of chopping motion. It cracks the softened exterior of the reed without damaging the fibres. Then you strip off the broken pieces of reed. You now have the makings of a textile that the women mostly, but sometimes the men, spin together and roll up on wooden spools. It is coarse and white in colour and when you have enough, you take it to town and someone who knows how to do it—how do you call it?—the tailor, will make you a shirt or a pair of pants. There is a big sheet of it in *Nonno's* garage covering the back seat of his van. I will later rescue it from such an ignoble and mundane, but typical, use.

My translation is rough and I look in desperation for Maria but she is off walking with her two *Zie*. The evening arrives and there is no time to panic. I must pace myself.

"Nicola, do you remember the *mangina*?" I ask, pointing my finger to my temple. I make a chopping motion with an imaginary handle held by my right hand brought down on my left arm. I am so pleased with the fluid rhythm of my *Inglese*, international sign language. Even the children stop to watch me.

Nicola stares at me, head cocked in avian inspection.

"The *mangina*," I say again, repeating the industrious motion.

Nicola looks helpless and holds out his arms.

Suddenly, a curious mixture of embarrassment and frustration shudders through me. I am not able to explain myself and I feel dumb.

"I hate it when your father plays the dumb Italian," I complain angrily to Mary. It is an expression I sometimes utter when I am shopping with the old guy. I see the look of impatience, of vague contempt on store-people's faces, I know what they are thinking and I want to throttle them. *Garibaldi* suddenly appears older and so unsure during these interactions. I want to protect him.

"The man is a king in his own household, an engineer, a politician, a grower of food, a mechanic, a carpenter, an artisan who can weave plastic gauge wire around countless demijohns. He is everyone's friend at the Club. He makes them little containers out of cereal boxes to hold their *scopa* and *briscola* cards. But when I am in a store with him he acts like a bumpkin, and I can tell they think he is stupid. God, does it ever bug me."

"What do you expect? He is old and they all talk too fast anyway," Mary says defensively.

The children fly off by now, chasing their attention like a butterfly. Later they tug at each other, turn in gladiatorial circles, and try to put one another through a *mangina* machine. I continue to reflect, for the enchantment has not yet passed.

I remember *Garibaldi* telling me about his first job in Toronto. He is young, with two kids. He and Lina are sponsored by *Zia* John and they have a debt to pay for their trip over. There is the rent and there is the food to buy.

"My first job?" he says pausing to remember. "My first job in this country did not work out. I did not know the language. I did not know where anything was. Somebody told me about a job in Scarborough. It was picking *fungi*—how do you call it?—the mushrooms. I got up early and they showed me how to get on the streetcar and I took it all the way out from Montrose Street near College. That is where we used to live. When I got there, they told me, "No, there are no jobs here." Then I had to find my way back. It is hard finding your way back when you don't know the way. I had my address on a little piece of paper. There was a lot of pressure: a family to feed, bills to pay, and the debt for the room and the furniture and the boat. That was our life then."

It is easy to understand his lesson. It is hard to be alive inside, so happy, so full of things to say, so wanting to let people know what you think and how you feel—about them, about what you see—wanting to converse with a hunger to be understood, to give and to get a joke, to feel sharp and shiny, not dull and blurry. "*Non puoi giudicare il libro dalla copertina.*" You can't judge a book…

"When we were at your Mom's old house, I felt like a dumb Inglese trying to talk with Nicola. I attempted to tell him about the *mangina* machine and I felt like a monkey," I say sadly to Mary.

She listens.

"At least I can speak *scopa*," I add, trying to salvage some pride.

"And *benezene*," she says, her eyes looking like wells.

Nicola seems to understand the moment and in his hand is a single green fig. It is what he went to search for at the back of the house. Fig season came early this year and the tree on the property at the back still had one robust straggler hanging on for dear life. He presents it to me and gestures with his hands for me to eat.

"*Mangia.*"

"*Magnifico!*" I say, holding it in my finger tips. I inspect the honey-gold interior of the half that is left.

"*Grazie*, Nicola."

"*Prego*," he says. And then he is off to see something else.

Maria comes around the edge of a stand of trees. She walks slowly, arm-in-arm with her two ancient aunts. The sun turns honey-gold and I see it in their squinting faces, the orange and red around them, the play of white and shade on the house behind. Two generations. Two sisters and a daughter to a fourth who is no longer here. The moment is revealing. I see how my wife will look in thirty years and I find my head cocked in avian inspection, made happy by this ancient vision.

The feminine entourage picks its way slowly along the side of the house, past the vines and out to the front. The children notice. They dart back in our general direction and emerge in front of us, with a laugh, beside the cars.

The ancient *Zias* are coaxed into front seats. The resolute slam of doors, the turn of engines, and we drive back down the winding road. In a moment there is wine and chicken, meat and pasta, orange pop, bread, *lasagne* and beans, melon and *espresso*, *liquore* and a full tour of the interior and exterior of Angelo's modern and beautiful home.

In the dark, at an unknown time, *la famiglia Vagabondi* wind their way down the street past the *pizzeria*, past the monument, around the corner from the little *piazza*, down the steps and through the narrow courtyard to our little house. I fumble with the lock, fumble again and soon, the libretto gives way to a melody of prone dreams.

***

87

All at once, I pile big red *Canadese* suitcases into the back of Domenico's car. It is time to go. Biagio takes Maria and the kids. Domenico and I follow with the luggage. We take the back way to Boiano, about twenty-five minutes away. There, we will take the train to Rome, find a hotel and then fly home the next day. Domenico expertly wends his way over and around, up and down the narrow roadways.

"*Dio*, Domenico. How can you see?" I say pointing to my sunglasses and then to the road.

I wear sunglasses and there are still parts of the road I can't see. He wears no sunglasses and it doesn't seem to matter. He takes each hairpin turn miraculously, without hesitation. It is a gift, I think.

"Choo," he replies matter-of-factly.

Too soon we pull into the train station in Boiano. Biagio is beside us. There is the flurry of getting out the bags, clicking up the little handles and rolling them to the train platform. It is deserted and has that war movie feel. The kids go to explore and we stand around with the downcast hesitation that leaving brings. Suddenly, to my left, at the corner of the station I notice movement and colour and then there is noise and triumphantly Nina, Salvatore, Marica, Enrica, Noemi, Kristina, Valentina, Gabriele and Ester spill out onto the platform!

There are hugs and touch and kisses and before I know it, Salvatore leaves and returns with tiny Styrofoam cups of *espresso*.

"*Chin chin!*" we say.

The train announces its arrival and suddenly it wheezes to a stop. *Shhhhhhh.* There is no time now. We all cry and hoist red *Canadese* bags onto the train. A whistle trills the chill of departure right through our hearts. The hugs and kisses are quick now and I find Biagio last.

"*Grazie*, Biagio, *Your famiglia e bella! Molto, molto bella!*"

He laughs and replies in dramatic English, "Goodbye. See-You-Soon."

"*Ahh! Si Si!*" I say.

And we are gone.

In the *cantina* I take a long hard pull from the plastic siphon tube and completely fill my mouth. I remove the tube and slide my index finger off the end so it will stream into the old whiskey bottle and fill it to the cap line. I return to the table. I sit with *Garibaldi* and he smiles.

"I can't believe how kind everybody was. It was so overwhelming. I could not pull my wallet out. I tried it once in the little *piazza* and Nicola got cross with me. I had to sneak away and buy treats for the kids when we went over to Domenico's for dinner. Nicola and I had a big *scopa* tournament with your brother and Nico. We completely destroyed them. Then I beat Nicola and gave him the set of cards you gave me. He even has an official cereal box case," I say with a flourish.

"And you won't believe this but I tell you it is true," I continue. "On the airplane coming back, sitting behind us was a family with two kids. They were coming from Boiano! It was their first time to Canada. They were supposed to meet the mother's uncle. Mary helped them with the passport lady, showed them where to get their bags and translated for the customs guys. It was so beautiful."

"That's good," he nods.

"But I tell you this," I repeat. "It frightens me to think what a huge loss it would be, if we did not take your *nipote* to see the Home-town—to see a part of their heritage. A man should not miss his chance!" I bang the table once to emphasize the *lezione*.

"Yes." *Garibaldi* says simply, pouring out the heel of the bottle into my glass. He winks and I drain it in one go.

Act III

[Act III]

Scene 1.

Canto Primo

Il Vagabondo *meets* Garibaldi *for the first time*

I turn onto Rita Drive in North York. The first thing I see is the church in which we will be married next year. The road curves around sharply past the house with the little *Jesu* shrine on the front lawn, the one attached to the house where no one is ever home. I see the next set of paired dwellings and I won't remember a thing about the people two doors down. They are from a different era. Beside them is a Black Madonna. She is aware already that I am slowing down. I wheel into the driveway and look fully at the dark, inquisitive scrutiny, the penetrating, slightly worried gaze that signals the presence of a stranger. I am sure when I get out of the car that if there is a dog on the property it will kill me. I look up to say hello and the Black Madonna is gone. Later I will understand that she has gone in to get a better look. The driveway is pristine. There are no oil spots on it, nothing that would suggest debris. It pulls up to a white apron of clean, white concrete that is the threshold, alternately to the garage and to the side door next to the *cantina*. A blue Dodge Caravan on the left stands parallel to the little red brick wall which is topped with cement. And bordering that, in a proud, cascading row is a garden of tiny pink flowers, bobbing snap dragons and solid red roses. These are presided over by a plastic lion in repose and two plastic hens in laying form. Each of them has a red geranium growing out of its back. A garden fork rests its tines at a jaunty, well used angle. Shade hovers over the steps that lead up to the front door and then, down and around to the side yard which, I will later see, opens to the backyard and the garden and the yard barn and the makeshift greenhouse and the compost, cleverly buried next to the foundation. Later, I will meet the other backyards crowding around gaily, as if they are all at a festival. This is where I will spend all of my summer, spring and fall and very soon I won't really want to stay indoors there, except in the downstairs kitchen, to eat. There are two trees. Thankfully, I can tell the large one is a pear tree. I will later be told, upon asking, that the second tree is a peach tree. Their shadows play on a tiny strip of grass that rolls slightly down to a hedge, boxed neatly at right angles.

To the left of the trees, I notice a woman on the property next door. She gets up and comes down the stairs to the side yard. She takes her time.

"How do you do?" I smile and call out nicely.

She smiles and nods her head several times. She wipes her hands on her apron and continues down her side yard to her backyard. Her side yard is a thin parade ground with two pear trees and an apple tree standing first watch. I will later come to understand the leafy marching orders and note that any tree that is not a fruit tree is relegated to the tiny strip of grass owned by the city, next to the street.

I am aware now of a third pair of eyes. They watch me from inside the garage at the front. They are the eyes of the—how do you say it?—the father. He is at the work bench when I drive in, busy with something. He looks over his shoulder and then turns his back on me. He looks again and I can see he is setting something down and reaching for one of those red-orange gas station cloths. Something has registered. Perhaps I have driven over the black hose and tripped an imaginary bell. There is no rush. He turns and for a subtle moment faces me without moving. Because I am standing still, I can see moods cross the Italian face with the speed of clouds moving across a bright blue sky. First there is the imposed concentration of work, then a transition to disorientation, then a focusing and realization of what you are seeing and finally, the first opinion moves out to see what will happen next. He is wearing his blue overalls and a solid pair of work shoes. Already, he has a deep tan, made deeper by the white sleeveless undershirt framed in an unbuttoned blue vee. His hair is grey. He has a prominent nose, not unlike his daughter's. He has that healthy, outdoor look that old guys sometimes get, along with the fluid paunch that grows big in the winter when there is less to do and flattens out in the spring and summer when there is everything to do.

"How do you do?" I say, stepping across the threshold, offering first my hand and then my name.

Later I will say to Mary, "Geez. Between Maddalena, Margherita and your Dad (*old guy*), I might just as well have yelled out 'Hi everybody! By now you can tell I am a complete stranger, not Italian, probably not a Catholic and some sort of English guy who has come to see Angelo's Italian daughter. How's everybody doin' today?'"

Mary replies by laughing and hiding her face in both hands. I note the more I come around, the more I will see this gesture. It translates as dialect for "I-hope-you-will-still-be-here-when-I-open-my-eyes."

Angelo Molinaro says hello to me and returns my hand.

There is silence.

Lesser men might look to be rescued, run away or be angry later on. By the time I am saved by Mary who, thankfully, has come as quickly as she could, I am able to tell her that the second tree is a peach tree; that her Dad has a fine wine press but one of the slats needs replacing and that a demijohn holds approximately five cases of grapes, depending on the year and how much juice you can get from them. You will need to top them up to keep the cork moist. I am also pleased to note that "the Father" smokes Export A's and I am able to communicate, through gesture, my own penchant for Player's Plain, once enough time has passed and I am not so at-attention.

Several years later, *Garibaldi* will simply announce in his resolute fashion that he quit smoking. He keeps the unopened pack of cigarettes in his shirt pocket for a while. It migrates to a wooden box in the garage and twenty years later I will find it unopened when we are packing him up. But for now, I am somewhat at ease noting you can cover a lot of silent ground sharing a smoke. I am careful to finish mine in second place so I can see where he is going to put his butt. I follow him out to the road and return with him to the garage.

"Daddy, this is the one I was telling you about. We go to school together downtown," Mary says.

She helps to turn me into an entity in her father's mind and I can actually see him put the idea together like a hose on a faucet, trying it out, examining the threads. Couple it. Uncouple it. Couple it. Uncouple it. Set it down. Walk away. It is a strange thing to be with these Italians. At first you don't even have a presence, as if you are not or will not even be there in a second. Later when you are there and the enchantment pervades, you will be both visible and invisible—loved either way. You are alternately there and if you are not there, they know where to find you. It is called la *famiglia*.

"Mamma says it is time to get ready to wash up for lunch," she adds.

Quietly, I brace myself for the next meeting and before I know it, I am inside the house. I have slipped off my shoes and I am given a pair of slippers. It is an oddly informal gesture that chips away a bit of my tension. I am shown how to wash up at the utility sink near the furnace in the basement, where to hang the towel on the line strung indoors across the low ceiling'd room and finally, where to sit at the downstairs kitchen table. There I meet Lina. After I am enchanted I will know her as Pasqualina Maria Christina Molinaro, née Mascitelli.

"Mamma, this is the one I was telling you about at school," is the way I am again introduced, only this time, it is *parle Italiano*.

"*Buongiorno, Signora,*" I say, getting the time of day off by an hour or so. "Very nice to meet you."

She is small, with a beautiful smile and grey hair that becomes her. Her eyes are worried in the corners and wet-black and I can see that I have been taken in fully, quietly inspected and returned, smoothed out and a little less wrinkled. It is not unpleasant to be returned that way. I sit next to Mary across from her mother, comforted by the sense of intimacy when all else around me, the sight, the sound, the smell and then the tastes are so foreign. Behind me is where the plate from the Bahamas will go, brought back for them as a souvenir from our honeymoon. To my left at the opposite head of the table is Carmine, Mary's brother. He is amused at the whole thing, alternately serious and grinning, and I have a sense that I am passing a certain early muster. He lives at home but will triumphantly move out to Brampton as I begin to come over more and more.

Later, he will have a word with me in the garage to the effect that his sister is very important to him and that it is equally important that she does not, how does he say it? get "jerked around" by wrong-meaning guys.

"I am smarter than I look," I say to Mary later on, outside, after she removes her head from her hands and stops laughing. "I can see that they love you."

It is one of the *lezione* from the early days before I enter the Court of *Garibaldi* and well before the insights into the ancient order and the systems of hillside flames. Later, I will understand that even the young think they know, but they don't know. They think they are free or need to be free of the ancient order but it is turning in gyres within them, slowly, like the languid airborn twist of a hawk, like the deliberate motion of a wine press, or the oil-vinegar-salt-toss rhythm of salad preparation. You cannot escape your parents. Go with the motion and you will feel your stubble burning off, offered up in white-smoke open air cathedrals on hillsides. Go against it and you will suffer because you reject the way you are meant to follow.

My stomach turns my mind to the stove and I must already be under a certain spell because I see two motions that will always intrigue me—two motions that I will copy again and again and again until I enter the state of *gusto*. When you feel the languid enchantment, you have already understood the word *felice* in your heart. It rolls off your tongue like meat sliding off a rib into a pool of bubbling, thick red sauce on glistening steaming pasta, smothered in grated dry Asiago cheese and sprinkled, against unbelievable protest, with salt and pepper for you are an *Inglese*, heart and soul, loved in *Garibaldi's* Court.

"*No!*" you hear them say. "*Sele? Pepe? No, No, No!!!! Dio*"

"*Felice. Fe-lee-chay. Fe-leee-chay,*" you say over and over to yourself.

You breathe in fully, you put your left hand on your heart, you throw your right hand with abandon out into the operatic life and you sing the libretto.

There is a silver beauty to a boiling pot of water. The waiting, the awakening hiss as molecules heat up, soon to begin their tumble; the first bubbles past the tipping point and the whole thing speeds up now boiling fiercely with spatters escaping to *shish* off the burner. Then you know it is time to slide the pasta in. *Penne rigate. Penne rigate!* It heaps stiffly at the bottom and quickly quiets the surface of that happy sea. Steam rises in anticipation, there is the hissing and then presto! The whole thing takes off again. This is when you pour the salt, at first into the palm of your left hand, but later, when you know the lesson, directly into the steaming boil. You are a fool if you put the lid on now and walk away because you will boil the whole damn thing over and you will reluctantly pull the burners out, the pans they sit in, soak and scrape off the mess. This is the precise moment to stay, to watch and then to enter into the thrall of the enchantment. Pick up the plastic spoon and slowly, lovingly begin to turn the pasta. Watch them soar around in scalding bliss and grow quietly thicker. They swirl and swirl hypnotically and soon you will notice that you are stirring them absentmindedly, gently, still lovingly, while your mind blends into warm steam. It is like being read to when you watch it being done. Then when you are ready—there is no rush— step back. Pull off the green leaves of lettuce, tear them into jagged shapes and let them tumble into the bowl. Run your fingers through them. Lift them. Roll them. Cut up the wet tomato into irregular cubes and place their moist weight on the salad leaves. The cucumber is next, spilling into the cracks left by the tomatoes and leafy greens. Always slice up an onion into thin, curving petals, wipe your hands on a tea towel and then return to the pasta to maintain the fluid, spinning motion. The next sequence is the best. Pick up the bottle of extra virgin olive oil, Bertozzi, Colavita or Rastrelli if you can find it, and pour it on the salad in a slow, steady, circular fashion, from the centre to the circumference. Pour it again. Step back. Now you remove the lid from the wine vinegar and circle the bowl in a different motion. Stop. Erratically shake salt over the entire thing. Stop. Circle with wine vinegar and Stop. Toss the *insalata* now, gently with spoons. Stop. Add more wine vinegar and because you are possessed, a bit more salt. Taste. If you do it right you will be enchanted. If you close your eyes and say *Felice* like you mean it, you will notice that the fingers of your right hand will come together at the tips; that they will turn towards your heart and they will gently match the rhythm of its beat. It is a gift.

Scene 2.

Overture to a Side Yard.

Garibaldi *holds court*

Dinner is done and like a true *Inglese*, I get up to help clear the plates. There are protests from Mary's mother.

"It's okay, *Ma*," I hear her say.

Incredibly, I start to rinse them at the sink and before I know it, Lina is standing beside me. She gently, but resolutely takes the tea towel from my grip. Silently, Mary joins her. The quiet ring of fork tines and the efficient clack of porcelain pronounce the end of dinnermass and I sort of take it that I am to leave the kitchen and follow Angelo outside. It is all unspoken and there is no rush. Carmine has disappeared.

Outside in the garage, I try to find something to do to arrest the silence. I offer him a smoke. Thankfully, he takes me up on my offer. We stand at the mouth of the garage, exhaling strongly. Our eyes sweep the street, first up and then down. I feel him standing beside me. The silence seems to create an electric current in the space between us and I know I will get a shock when anybody speaks. I put my hand in a pocket to ground myself.

An old woman in dark clothes walks towards the church.

"*Ciao*, Angelo!" she calls out from the sidewalk. "*Come sta?*"

"*Non c'e male*," he gestures with a shrug.

A small man and woman, the man in a tweed jacket, the woman in a shawl, head north in an ambling waddle, weighed down by yellow bags of groceries from Valencia. Valencia is just south of Rita, at the crossroads. It is a mysterious place. I go there on my own for the roast potatoes, the meat, the cheese—everything! Angelo eyes the old couple intently. They look over and wave. He waves back. The woman's eyes take me in and I see her turn her head towards the husband.

We walk out to the road and pitch our butts into the gutter.

A horn beeps and there is Rocco driving by, grinning.

Angelo grins back. Reflexively, I wave.

He offers me an early *lezione* at passing time but I don't know it yet and neither does *Garibaldi*. Later, when I learn to sing the libretto of his Court, I will realize that it is my first introduction to his street and to his neighbourhood, but for now, I could be anywhere in North York. I cannot hear the music of that place or sing the libretto, nor can I see the flames on the side of its mountain.

"He is showing me things even then," I will say to Mary, years later when insight strikes and lights up my thoughts.

"He can't help it," she will reply proudly.

The side door stretches open with a relieved metallic sigh and Mary calls us in for coffee.

We come in, slip off our shoes and I put on the brown slippers for the second time. It is a good sign.

I see small oranges, rosy nectarines, apples and green grapes in a bowl. There is a plate of strange looking cookies, hard round ones, with nuts sticking in them and ridged ones in the shape of an "S". A medium-sized, faceted steel pot sits on an oven mat and I am poured coffee into a tiny cup. I watch the old guy take his little spoon and put in some sugar and I follow suit. The thick, smooth taste startles me. It is perfect.

"It tastes beautiful!" I say to Lina, not even getting the English right.

She smiles, nods and nudges the cookie plate in my direction.

Later, when I am enchanted, this offertory will take on legendary proportions. Because of her, time after time, I will pass a plate to my dinner guests. I will look deeply into their eyes. I will intrude upon their personal space and with a proud, dramatic inflection in my voice and a seriously pained frown upon my face, I will gesture and simply say:

For me. Take one. For Me.

We will laugh out loud, uproariously so. Mary will shake her head and I will profess my love in proper order for my two Italian women and for them alone. It is the way of *Il Vagabondo*! *Cosi sia.*

Happily, unbelievably some might say, the two young people are excused and Mary says to her mother, "Ma, we are going outside."

The front door sighs open and seals shut and we turn quickly right to go up the cement steps, underneath the pear and the peach trees to lift the latch and swing open the gate to the side yard. There is time to hold hands, to laugh and to kiss so we do. By the time we reach the side door and the windows to the kitchen, we cleverly walk beside one another. It is only then that Mary remembers to look back, over towards Maddalena's side window to see if the coast is clear. Our hands clap over our mouths and we hunch over giggling to make our careless way for two lawn chairs spread out by the yard barn. We put up our feet.

It is here, in *Garibaldi's* side yard, next to his garden, in the back that I am seriously taught to pass time. I will show it to you. In order to pass time, you must be sitting. It is better if your feet are up but this is not totally necessary. There is no rush. If you do it right you will enter a precise space where there is no immediate memory of past and no immediate thought of the future. There is nothing to do next. It is unnecessary to speak or to engage in conversation. I have passed time with as many as six people at once and not said a single word. If you are lucky and there is a cherry tree in your backyard and if it is cherry season you can pick an entire handful of gleaming berries and fire the pits off into oblivion between the thumb and index finger of your right hand. Later if you have children, you can spit them at each other from your chairs and laugh until you can't take it any more. If you do this to pass time, it is unhelpful to wear white. If there is a silver dollar plant growing in the spaces left over in the side yard by the potatoes, the beans, the strawberries, the onions, the orégano, the basil plants, exiled from the garden, you can pluck off the perfectly round, wafer thin green blossoms (or whatever you call them) and carefully peel them apart to free the black seeds inside. The black seeds must be counted either to yourself or against whoever is passing time with you. The wise seed counter is careful not to remove too many blossom-pods. It is possible to pass time for up to two hours but if you have to count, or if when you get up, you feel guilty or are worried about the time, you are not enchanted and have not passed time properly. So, try to do it again. This is all I know about it. It is a hard lesson to learn and an easier lesson to forget, especially for the young and modern.

I recline now. There is time to gaze. Mary and I talk and then do not talk. It is the aimless cadence when we are growing comfortable and love takes its first, gentle hold. My eyes sweep across the clean, squared concrete patio that I will later learn is poured perfectly by Orlando, next door. He is a Calabrese. He is intense. Sometimes I see his distracted, troubled look when he concentrates on something, and yes, there is a sort of seismic shudder to the man but at least you can feel it coming. To me, he is friendly and I like him. The concrete is between the back of the house and the garden and runs along the side yard, pulling everything into clean and tidy definition. The ribbed rebar that is not already put to use in the garden is carefully stored beside the yard barn and the neighbour's fence. The foundation of the house is painted grey. The foundation next door is painted grey. The foundation next door to that, on the other side, is painted grey. It is the same for the other three fellows in the back. As far as my eye can see, the grey never peels and it always looks freshly painted. It is a curious connection and the movement of my eyes from foundation to foundation to foundation unlocks the enchantment. Suddenly I see, carefully, each vibrant garden.

"Everyone does it their own way."

Vincenzo's tomatoes are supported by six-foot tripods of wooden stakes. He has an oven and later, I will taste his pizza. AnnaMaria gives me a jar of small, hot red peppers bathed in oil and stuffed with olives. Dante is a *maestro* at growing zucchini. There is one plant originating two doors down. Incredibly, it travels along all the back fences, throwing its arms around every yard as it grows in green embrace. It is magnificent. Between Margherita, Franca, Maddalena, and Lina I will bring home hundreds of zucchini. Each one of them, so graciously accepted but years later I will confess to Mary, "You know, Mary, I never really knew what to do with all those zucchinis. We never ate them and they are not that good, raw."

"And you ate canned spaghetti, too," she reminds me.

The guilt of looking into so many beautiful Italian women's faces and accepting Ferlisi bag after Ferlisi bag of foot-long, two-foot-long, three-foot-long zucchinis tears me apart. Ferlisi is our other store, just across the road from Valencia, on the north side. She is *importante*, like someone from the Hometown, like a—how do they call it?—a *paesana*.

"*Dio! Grazie signora, Grazie, no, per favore, Grazie, no. Prego, arrivederci, ciao!*"

"You will not die from this!" is the early *lezione* and later I will make a determined point to go to Zucchini Soup School as penance.

I do not drop out. Lina is my *professore*. I hear the clicking of the igniter on the little gas stove in the basement kitchen: *ffoooff*. I trim the beautiful blue flame to low. The entire *lezione* is taught to me through demonstration ("This is the only way to learn"), primarily in *Italiano* with a few *Inglese* concessions. I will do my best to pass it on to you.

First you must find a paisley apron that zips up the front. Put it on while the frying pan is heating up. You want to protect your clothes because this makes the laundry go easier. Add to the pan a thin layer of olive oil, Rastrelli if you can find it. Colavita is also fun to say and may be used. Finely chop a *cipolla* (*onion*) and sauté. Add some—*come si dice?—come si chiama?—string beenz*. Slice your zucchini thinly. Leave the skin on. (*Dio*, it is not a cucumber, what are you thinking?) Place the beautiful zucchini in a pot, cover with water, bring to a boil. Add finely cut *potate e sedano* (*celery*) *e prezzemolo* (*parsley*). You will be amazed to learn that there is another kind of parsley that is not *Inglese*. It has always been there but you have not seen it. When you are enchanted you will see it. Salt to taste. Now that it is boiling, add the sautéed *cipolla e* green beans. *Perfetto!* Make a chopping motion in the air, next to your cheek and say to your mother in law; that is, the Italian standing next to you, in a firm, definitive voice: *Abbi pazienza!* and if you purse your eyebrows and stand too close, you will get a smack.

After twenty or so minutes—there is no rush—crack *due uovi* (see "Berlitz: if-you-speak-English -you-can-speak-Italian Self Teacher book. "*You should know this by now, what are you a testa dura?*") into the pot and give them ten minutes or so to mix into the *zuppa*. You are a *burlone* if you do not add the pepper now. Serve steaming in bowls with crusty air-filled *Italiano pane* crumbling *Asiago* cheese *e vino.* "Now, you know."

There is a breeze. Sheets are drying everywhere. Air conditioners hum. Bees float by and then accelerate off into oblivion. I truly enjoy Margherita's use of long tree branches to stake her tomatoes. They bring a new texture to this open air *fresco.* I am about to mention this to Mary, who by now is fully and expertly passing time, when, suddenly, we hear the gate *clank.* We look up to see Angelo entering the side yard. He walks towards us. His tanned handsome face looks serious. There is a sensation of shadows growing longer as he towers over us and then stands there.

"Hi, Daddy!" *Garibaldi's* daughter says, looking up.

"Hello, Angelo," I say. "Your garden is beautiful."

"There is some things I have to say," he starts out plainly.

I sit up in my chair.

"My wife and I know."

"Daddy! don't—" Maria begins to interject.

"My wife and I know," he continues, "that you are coming around now, but I have to tell you. I don't know if I like you. I don't know if I don't like you. I just don't know you, that's all."

There it is. Nothing more needs to be said.

But Angelo's daughter is short with her father, the way daughters are, and I stand now, amazed.

"How did you first meet Lina?" I say to him, to cheer him up, one night around the kitchen table. *Il Vagabondo* drops in on him regularly now.

"You never know when you will see me and that way I will be sure to find some food!" I say with a flourish, when he opens the door, surprised to let me in.

"It was different then, than it is now," he begins. "In Italy, when you got engaged, it was not like you go to the girl's house, pick her up and go around. Over there, you went to the girl's house. You sat there. Her mother sat there. The father sat there and the girl sat over there so far away from you. There was no way you could get close to her to talk. If you had to talk, you had to talk through the parents, to the family, where everyone was sitting. That's the way it was," he says, remembering.

"So how do you know if the girl likes you?" I say.

"*Mmmm*. You found a way to figure that out," he says.

"And?" I say tumbling my left hand around and around in front of me. This is not an Italian gesture; rather I am using my hand with *Garibaldi* in the *Inglese* dialect, so as to encourage him to pick up the pace. It is a fault of the young, I know.

Garibaldi ignores me and continues in the slow gait of memories being called over to talk.

"You see, over there, what you did was, you wrote a little note to the girl, telling her about your feelings. When she got the note, she wrote a note back, to say if she agreed with you or not. Most of the time, the girl would say, 'No, I am too young for that.' So then you'd say, 'That's OK' and you wrote a note to someone else.

"What happened to me was this," he says now fully recognizing his memories and embracing them. "I wrote a note and gave it to her girlfriend to give to her. That girlfriend told her boyfriend to tell me she already had a boyfriend, that they were engaged and that I should have nothing to do with them. The same story was going around in the town. So I sent a note directly to my wife to see what she had to say about it.

"The answer I got was that she was too young and couldn't get engaged yet. She was seventeen years old." So I said: "OK, OK, forget about it!" Here, *Garibaldi* claps his hands and makes a motion like he is wiping them off. I can tell he is using the Molise hand dialect so I slap the table for emphasis, teasing him.

"*No*," I say. "It is impossible!"

"But how we got really engaged was through another friend of mine that was engaged to my wife's cousin's daughter," he continues, ignoring me. "They were family, so my friend came around to tell me that if maybe I insisted, I would get engaged. But I had another problem. My in-laws didn't like me."

"That's not possible," I say genuinely. "Why?"

"Because they had some property and we had nothing, that's why. That is the reason!" he says clapping his hands resolutely in the air like the thing is final; like it is done. It is one of those complete gestures that says everything at once.

"Did they tell you they don't know if they like you, like you said to me?" I ask, calling over a few memories of my own as if they were on my property, loitering.

"No," he says. "It's not that they didn't like me. It was a difference of position. The position they were and the position we were."

"So how did you resolve it?"

"The friend that was engaged to my wife's cousin's daughter started something going around and he said to me again, 'Angelo, if you insist, you might get something there.'

"He was giving me a tip but I am stubborn and I have been stubborn since I was born. So I said, 'No. To heck with it. I don't want to do anything about it!'"

"But my friend," he persisted, "he said to me, 'I tell you what you could do.' There was a *festa* in town, with a band, in the *piazza* in front of the church. I was going around with the people to have a good time. My friend said to me: 'Watch! She is looking after you everywhere you go!'

"But I said to him, 'When I get something refused, I don't push for it, so forget about it.'

"'Angelo,'" he said, "'can't you see it?' He got between me and my stubbornness and he forced me to try."

"*Come si chiama?*" I say.

"Donato Macoretta," he says.

"Well then, Donato Macoretta is my friend!" I say resolutely.

"So I speculated on that," he continues in memories now full friends. "I told Donato, 'You go and tell your girlfriend to tell her if she wants to talk to me, she has to come behind the church.'"

"Sounds like a side yard to me?" I say, smartly, but he doesn't get it.

"So she met me and I asked her if the answer she gave me was because she was too young to get engaged, or because she was engaged to that guy."

"She says: 'No, I am not engaged to that guy, but my parents don't want me to get engaged with you.'"

"Why?" I say, fully entranced by the living opera.

"She said, 'My parents got a little more than what you got because you haven't got anything.'"

"She said that?" I ask, in disbelief.

"Yes," he says proudly. "So I asked her: 'What about you? Do you want to get engaged with me or not?'"

"'Yes,' she said, 'but my parents—'"

"So I said: 'Tell your parents that I am going to come and see you at your home—at the farm.'"

"It was on a Saturday night!" I interject, remembering this fragment of the story. "People were busy every other night, but on Saturday you could go," I say triumphantly.

Garibaldi looks at me intently and then his memories invite him back into the conversation.

"That's right," he says. "When I went there, I knocked and both parents came to the door. At first the father said, 'What do you want?'"

"I bet you he was nicer than you were to me," I say, trying to set the bait.

"Didn't Lina tell you I was coming?" he continues, ignoring the bait.

"'Yes. She told me. But what do you want?'"

"So I told them about it. They were on one side of the door and I was on the outside."

"Her father asked me: 'So what have you got to offer her?'"

"'Well,' I said, 'the only thing I could offer her is my love. Other things I haven't got.'"

"So the father said, 'Well, I have to think about it. You go home and we'll talk about it another time.'"

Angelo is laughing now.

"Wow!" I say, shaking my head incredulously. "Now I can see why you put me through the ringer!" I am laughing too.

"So when did he say, 'OK, you can marry my daughter'?" I ask finally.

"That was later on," *Garibaldi* says. "About *twothree* months. I went there almost every Saturday night. The first night I couldn't get on the farm. Then they let me in and they told me: You sit here. The mother sat here. The father sat there. And she was sitting way over there!"

"Bravo!" I say, clapping. It is a beautiful performance.

"And do you remember what I said to you?" I say, suddenly pushing my way into the midst of his memories, bringing them all back to the side yard and his concern on the first day.

"Yes," he says simply.

"I said, 'Well, Mr. Molinaro, I am going to make sure that you like me then!'"

"Bravo!" He smiles.

And later, when it is time—there is a rush—and I am nervous, I will seek him out alone, in the garage. Mary will be inside with her mother. In a choreography of love and respect I will tell him that I believe in God; that by now, I hope, he should be able to tell that I am a—how do they say it—a good man; that we go good together and that I would like his permission to marry his daughter. When I go inside, I am careful to see that there is more twinkle than worry in Lina's eyes and that I am now a rich man. The old ways are good enough for me.

"*Nonno*'s mother-in-law loved him," I will tell the kids some time later. "One time, after he was married, there was a really bad snowstorm. They hadn't heard from *Nonna*'s parents for a week. There were no telephones back then so he walked all the way over to the farm. The snow was so deep, he couldn't get through, so he wrapped his long coat around himself and rolled down the lane like a big snowball and landed on their front door. When they saw him shake off the snow like a dog, it was like they came alive again.

"Bravo!" they will say, enchanted.

Scene 3.

The Garage. Winemaker's Tableau.

The life inside and the life outside

Time after time I enter the perfect place. The smooth floor has a clean shine. The smell could be called an aroma for there are wisps of the *cantina*, wisps of fresh air, wisps of grapes and pears and finally, wisps of clean, unused motor oil and the faint breath of varsol. Along one side hang the ladders, assorted cords and restrained bundles of rope against a clean backdrop of concrete block. Homemade brown cupboards huddle in the upper corner. They hold soldering irons, propane bottles, drills, a skill saw and a small working motor affixed to a board. There is a table saw tucked underneath, next to the back seat of the van. The seat is in exile from what I affectionately call—how do I say it?—the Italian pickup truck. It is covered in rough white cloth, made from extracted reeds cracked open by the *mangina* machine and spun from loom.

"How can you use something that important, that historic, on something where it will get that wrecked?" I ask one day, in the exasperation of carefully, measured, words.

"*Eh*," they say and gesture with a shrug. "We don't have much use for it now."

It is like that with them. Everything is used and then re-used, recycled and then used again in ways to make it ever more useful; or else it is given away to someone next door who can use it better. After that, there are the poor to think about and someone at the church or at Goodwill is called. Finally, when the last use is squeezed out, like juice from the *mosto*, it is discarded, thrown out and there are no second thoughts.

Eyes roam to the back of the garage and the detailed beauty of the homemade work bench, with primitive drawers that open smoothly and never jam. The pegboard is draped with clusters of tools, actual store-bought ones, mysterious ones and hybrids. The mysterious ones are used once a decade. I like to think of what they were used to fix and when they were purchased and why. But it is the hybrid tools that I love to look at and examine and hold in my hands. They are works of art and marvels of engineering. I see homemade screw drivers probably used to reach some long forgotten place, underneath a cowling or a manifold, back in the days when you could work on your own car and fix it. Ancient hammers with new handles. Curious looking awls transplanted into warm, antique pieces of wood. Concocted saws with strange thin blades screwed into even stranger pieces of steel. Long, smooth shovel handles attached to everything that can possibly be used to scrape or dig or shift or move. My favourite is the one with the wafer of sturdy metal grafted onto a smooth piece of oak. It is used, with precision and ease, to remove the ice from the front step by the *cantina*. If you are back at your house and you need a pry bar to remove a stump, there are two in the corner to choose from. If you need a toilet snake to unclog your plumbing, there is one coiled to the right. It is longer and more functional than anything you will ever find in the stores. You can always borrow the orange pruner or the shovel that will reach deep into post holes. Just make sure you return it or you will violate Rule G. The husbands will fuss and complain to their wives intermittently for weeks. Finally the wives will go and assertively retrieve the tools. They will make peace. And the amazing thing is, if the same neighbour comes to ask for another tool, he will be given it by the husbands who do not want to make a problem. This is also the reason why they need sons.

There is every known piece of wood in every needed shape and size wedged into the rafters above. Along the right hand wall, more curious homemade cabinets, little blocked-off spaces with small hinged doors that conceal every washer, nail, screw, bicycle cap or bolt you, or friends on the street will ever need. The garage in *Garibaldi's* Court is a place of pure solution. You can feel the sphere of concentration there. The *problemi*, the tinkering, the washing up for lunch, the return, the tenacity, the next day, the talking with a neighbour and the eureka-moments when the thing is fixed and it is time to down a glass of wine in one go ... the sequence is all there, inside singing and dancing like spirits at a feast. I can see them.

And in the corner, with its slats, its cogs and bars, its dark blocks of wood for ratcheting, the wine press stands stoutly on its cast iron base. It is Michelangelo's work right down to the iron indentations at the toes to keep the sculpture stable. It is an object that must be touched, must be turned, must be set up and used. Spirits are made from it. It is a truly masculine piece. There is no tug-of-war, no competition. No foolish infertile, androgynous arguments. It is because it is. It stands like a fruiting body. Below it a mycelium network of webs and fibres weave into the soil, the daily cycles and the seasons right back to the textured hillside across from the *Castillo*. It is planting. It is harvest. It is the burning of stubble. Carefully, those tendrils stretch across the valley and up the hillside into the town. They branch this way and that, silently linking family to family and men to men ending and beginning exactly beside Rosie's stall at the base of the ancient press. The Alpha and the Omega, yet it takes two to make a life because the women see it all strongly. They know what they know and what I will never know and can only guess at. There is a romance to the hard life. It is born from the unity that a division of labour creates. I have seen it. It is enchanting and I am smarter than I look.

It is late September and we go now to the corner of Jane and Sheppard, *Garibaldi* and I, to look at the grapes. It is morning, cold and bright. Yellow jackets float from crate to crate completely uninterested in you for they are intoxicated in the land of *uva per vino*.

The place is filled with old guys. They are small and wrinkled. Some of them smoke. There is laughing and loud talk. One or two young guys run the giant press or move crates around silently with propane fork lifts. The crates are pilled as high as your chest. You can get close to them. Smell them. Try each one: Muscato, Carrignane, Alicante, Montepulciano, Ruby Cabernet, Grenache. There is motion everywhere. Pull one of the wet brown leaves wedged in the purple blue sea and rub it with your fingers. Crumple it. There are new demijohns in plastic baskets. It is the beginning of the end of an era because they look so stylish compared to the slightly mildewed wicker containers, garishly woven in green, white, red and black ten-gauge electrical cord covering the dark green glass of *Garibaldi's* equipment. Plastic tubing, smart oak wine presses standing on thin metal bases painted forest green for the urban set. Stoppers and airlocks, jugs of strange and unknown volume … it's all there.

"These are the *kiki*," he demonstrates, picking up a cluster from a box of Alicante. "They must be close together. Tight-like. This is what you want to buy."

I ask about the white powder on the grapes.

"Ahh," he says. "It is the medicine they put on them. They are all green when they ship them. The medicine keeps them from going bad. It is not like the way we had it," he says resignedly.

Later, when we are back at home, having lunch with Lina, Mary and the kids, I will ask him about the old days. But first I will wash up. It will be cold and the furnace will rumble on. The children will be watching TV or playing with a few toys that we took over and left. When they are little, I see *Nonna* enchant them and bring out clothes pins for them to line up and count and drive and stack on the *ceramica*. She will put a little carpet down for them so the cold doesn't seep into their bones. If it does or it doesn't they will still have a *bit a luce* (a little bottle) of apricot or pear juice. She will toast some bread and make them a *San Danielle* mortadella sandwich with *Saputo* provolone cheese. Another day they will have a beautiful yellow *pollo zuppa*, with little pasta *stelline* and a few pieces of soft, tasty orange carrot. Whenever they want it, there is Nutella, the thick chocolate hazelnut lubrication that goes between bread. *Nonna*-food: it is their private little tale of gusto and enchantment spun with hugs and with kisses from only their *nonna*.

"I love you too much," she will say, not quite getting the English right.

"Thank you, *Non-na*," they will chime out of the side of their mouth, their bodies buried in squeeze.

I enter the kitchen before it is time and watch. The water is boiling. It is—how do they say it?—*gnocchi*. They take time to make. Boil some potatoes and mash them. Coat them with flour. Pinch them into little odd shaped crescents. Freeze them. Later, I will teach you how to make it even better, but the water is boiling now. It is translucent, milky with flour. I am there in time to see the salt go in. Stir it lovingly. Lift the top off the sauce and smell. Take the enchantment deep into your lungs—there is no rush. The sauce has been ready for the last half hour. The *gnocchi* will take *twenty* *twenty-five* minutes, it depends how you make it. Celery is on the table. Black olives roll in a bowl.

Again, I volunteer to fill the bottle of rugged red wine. The steel door of the *cantina* opens with a suction sound. Immediately I enter a micro-environment of different smells: the scent of vino, the scent of fruit, the scent of old, stained two-by-fours smelling vaguely of wine must. Smaller plastic blue barrels sealed tight, their contents slowly and steadily fermenting in tiny boil. If it is too cold, maybe there is a heater going on the top wooden shelf. There is a case or two of O'Keefe beer and not far from them, a bottle opener nailed into the wood. There is an old "Bubble Up" Seven-Up opener hanging against the wall if you need it for outside. The empties are gone. The yellow six-pack of Mio beside the white six-pack of Brio tells me that the Sicilian man in the truck made his efficient delivery this morning. He has a hard working look, thin, dark and sinewy. He is friendly enough but quick to make his stops and finish off Rita Drive as fast as it takes to finish his smoke. Before me, just below eye level, is a full gallon jug so I don't have to change it. It is a misfortune to have to change the wine when dinner is ready (*shrug shoulders here*). I am alone in the *cantina*. I pull the plastic tubing out and let the wine fill my mouth. There is nothing like it. Another quick, guilty pull and then I fill up the bottle. It is important to carry it with one hand under the base, as I have been shown.

Finally the *gnocchi* rise up to the surface of the boiling water. *Garibaldi* automatically sits in his spot and does not need to be called; the children do. Mary is already there helping to serve. As the children take their seats I watch my *maestra* at work. She lifts the luscious pieces out with a curious ladle that allows the water to drain back into the pot. She slides them into a large shallow bowl, covering its flower pattern with a measured determination that there is enough. Sauce is spread in loving circles on top. Steam rises while wine is poured for women who protest that you pour too much. No matter how much you pour, *Dio*! You have not left enough room for the Mio.

"*Abasta, abasta!*" Enough, enough! they cry.

"*Ehhh,*" we say, and shrug.

It is a ritual and by now the cheese is heavily dusted on top of the *gnocchi: romano e parmesan*, nice and dry, the drier the better because there is more taste. The children sit still, suddenly alert as the whole wide bowl is set before them. Motion is slowing. Meatballs, large ones filled with onion, basil and orégano sit in a separate bowl together with pork ribs, their meat barely gripping the bone. These are placed at the other end of *la tavola*. And finally the *pane* is placed in a basket. The women wipe their hands on their aprons or a tea towel and sit. Hand to hand, heads bowed, there is peace which suddenly gives way to noise and laughter, clacking plates, tines ringing and the robust conversation that is *gusto*. *Chin chin*.

In the garage the *uva per vino* await. Thirty cases Carrignane, thirty cases Muscato, ten cases Alicante, all stacked with the wine-maker's sparing cadence. The Alicante makes the wine nice and dark, not too light. Wasps and more wasps follow them back. They must be delirious, singing *Volare* like *Dino Martinelli* and laughing from *kiki* to *kiki*.

We come outside now. There are new fresh smells. Someone is burning wood. *Garibaldi* stacks his six fifty-gallon drums on top of concrete blocks to give the spigots a little elevation. The insides are rinsed and wiped clean. The only medicine he uses is the fresh air. His system is improved each year and by now he has his motor and his crusher mounted on a little H-frame. It fits perfectly over the drum to catch the crushed grapes. Underneath there are aluminium flaps flaring out to guide the grapes in. It is his modification. You must be careful not to slit your hand along its edge. .

"You do it once and you learn," he says to me busily bolting down a piece.

"Yes, but will the motor work this year?" I ask baiting him.

"*Ehhh*, it will work," he shrugs. "I fixed it."

"Technology!" I say, shaking my head and mimicking him. "You old guys, always on the go … can't be satisfied with the old ways.

Always have to—how do I say it?—improve on the situation."

"You think you know, but you do not know," he says, picking up on our routine.

"Ha, I am smarter than I look!" I will say, jabbing with a left. "I am surprised I have to remind you that you have forgotten already. Back in the old days we used to have a huge cement vat. We would dump the grapes in … oh, and by the way, they were better then, than they are now. Did I tell you about the blight, the—how do you say it?—the disease that destroyed the grapes in the *Mezzogiorno* in 1920? Everything was wiped out and we had to start over. Were you listening? … *Dio*. We would dump the grapes and the kids and everyone would go in and start pressing them with their feet. There was a little trough and a tap to catch the juice. We didn't make this much then. We made more," I say triumphantly.

Garibaldi is listening and his eyes are happy.

"Do you know what the wooden cask is called that we used to put the wine in? We call it a *centrali*. It is huge. They used to send you inside with a mop to clean it, don't you remember? Back then, we made enough for us but we had to sell the rest in town," I finish with a flourish.

"You are a *Vagabondo!*" he will say, declaring the fight over while moving to the press.

It is a good press with slats about three feet tall, banded and standing evenly on its cast-iron base. You can get them bigger or smaller. The cogs are well oiled and all the wooden blocks accounted for. This year he had to make a new slat. It stands out like me against the dark stained line of well broken-in ones. The metallic ratchet, tooth by tooth makes a good solid sound when you pull the steel lever. It is reliable.

Angelo starts to whistle quietly to himself.

It is time now to get into our work clothes. He, into his blue Toronto Transit Commission overalls, and I, into my father's white Field Aviation coveralls.

"Angelo, look, I am working without a net," I call out, spreading my arms magnanimously. It is our joke when eating pasta. You are a professional if you can wear a white shirt and eat pasta without getting an unforgiving red sauce stain on it. You are "working without a net." It is a daring feat. If you are successful you can be loud and brag. If you fall, you must brace yourself and duck your head because your wife does not have time to do the laundry all day. It is worth the risk.

"First, you have to take the leaves out and throw them over here," *Garibaldi* begins his instruction. He turns on the motor and the crusher starts rolling loudly.

"Then you pick up the grapes like this," he says hoisting the entire crate on his left shoulder. "You pull the grapes down like this and let them fall into the crusher. Do not put your hands in here or you will crush them," he yells to make himself heard.

Soon I have the rhythm down. The stray cluster pieces that plop onto the clean garage floor are few and easily thrown in with the rest. It becomes a matter of pride to do the job efficiently, perfectly in the repetitive cadence of hard work. We laugh at the growing stains on my white overalls and with each crate I look more and more like a well-used slat. For a time I think of nothing but crates and lifting and stacking the empty ones. It is cool and loud in the garage and Angelo checks the tension on the fan belt.

Inevitably, we will pause for a moment and turn off the motor. Guiseppe or Rocco will walk by, or some old fellow I have not met from two streets over. They will call out merrily above the din and enter the enchanted winery of the Court on Rita Drive. Like all Italian men, they will see immediately that there is work to be done and they will go to the job that needs doing first. It is a gift.

They are so friendly to me and say something to Angelo in Italian and they all laugh.

I grin happily and say something like, "Joe, your wife is going to kill you for working with your good clothes on, *aspetta,* let us do it!" But he won't listen, they never do, and the next thing you will see is that he has quickly shifted into his work-face, concentrating as he hoists a case of grapes like it was nothing. He doesn't even get his shirt dirty. Suddenly the work is done, the motor is off, the metallic rasp of the crusher stops and we stand there laughing. Magically, the door opens and there is a beaker of wine with the correct number of glasses on a tray.

"*Buongiorno,* Lina!" they all say in chorus. "*Come va?*"

"*Bene grazie,*" she will say and then disappear into the house.

I work hard with my Italians and I drink wine on early fall days, with crates stacked high, their thin lids tied with twine in bundles. You will never find a better kindling for your fireplace.

After a time, the men leave and we begin to press what we crushed.

"You take the crushed grapes from here and put them into the press," he says demonstrating the procedure. When it is this full you put on this part and then the blocks and then the cam and the iron bar goes though here. Every *oncewhile* you give it a good turn, like this," he says.

"I notice you give me all the hard jobs," I tease him. "You send me back with the wasps, you make me lift and pull this over here and that over there ... you are what do we call it? a supervisor," I say to him, cutting the air with my right hand angled in a chopping motion.

"It is the only way to learn," he says triumphantly.

In time—there is no rush—we are called in for *caffè* and "S" biscuits, maybe some smooth oval almonds (as many as you want—take more) and the *frutta* because it is always there. We will return to the garage to finish our work. We will run the *mosto* through a final pressing, stems and all, and drain that into a separate container to make vinegar. It depends how you like to make it. Some people omit this step. The moist, bunched debris we will cart out to the boulevard at the front of the house but some of it, not too much, will go into the compost minus the stems. Together we will tie down the thick sheets of polyethylene plastic over each drum and later, when I finally figure out what to give him for Christmas, we will carefully cut the plastic and fit in one air lock each.

"See, I have improved on your—how do you say it?—your *systemi*," I will brag. "I am smarter than you look."

"Maybe," he will say.

Finally, we will be done. We will peel off our overalls and I will be made to leave mine, against protests, for washing in the laundry room. I will examine my stained hands with a satisfied look and they will be wrapped around beautiful mortadella-filled bread, crumbling *Asiago* on the side and always a last glass of robust red wine that I will hoist and drain in one go with the old guy. We will stand, share a wink and I, *Il Vagabondo* and *mia famiglia*, will go home.

"Take your time going, but hurry back," I will teach him to say in the *Inglese* dialect.

The garage door opens with an electronic jerk and an even mechanical roll upwards. He has modified it of course, to open with the push of a button. (*It is like that with them, but I told you that already, weren't you listening?*) If you plant a seed upside down it will eventually right itself. If you plant the same seed in shade it will outsmart you and find its way towards the sun. If you do something a hundred times, there is a point where you will stop, tilt your head and say: how can I make this easier? I don't know how you say it in Italian, but I have been there before, during and after that question. It is something to watch and when you find yourself doing it, you truly cross over into *Garibaldi's* Court.

I tell you again: first you see the problem. Then you must inspect it and think about it. This may take a day or two. Then you will take a day to go to Canadian Tire or some other hardware store to buy one. If it does not fit—there is no rush—you take it back (*shrug shoulders here*). When you get the right one, you might glance over the instructions once but it is more important that you get the idea in your mind of how a thing should go. Once you see how it works and you try the pieces with your hands and have watched it going up and down inside your head, you install it. If you have to chip a little concrete or chisel out a little two-by-four to make it fit perfectly, all the better. It doesn't matter that you are old and go up on the step ladder yourself when no one is around. It is like the sauce or any other thing: when the job is ready to be done you must do it. Besides, you can always argue later that you gave away your old, wooden step ladder to Vincenzo for his cherry tree and bought a lighter aluminium one that is easier on your back to carry. Holy mackerel, you are making me nervous!

There is a hum and then a loud click when the garage door flattens out, over the rafters.

I cast off a shrug and say to him, "*Hummph,* back in my day we didn't have all these—how do you call them?—devices. You had to open these things by hand, with your legs and with your back. Now everyone is lazy. You call this progress?"

"You can open it next time!" he replies, already in fine form.

The day is cold and everything shivers; the peach tree, the *cantina,* the grey sky, me. Quickly, we are inside. The door clanks down and it hits the concrete with a practiced clunk as the interior light comes on. Immediately I hear warm, wet sizzling. It is steady, amplified-in-series across six drums. The percussion of fermenting wine hits your senses like no other sound.

"You have to keep the temperature the same," he instructs. "If you leave the garage door open too long, it will get cold and it will make the juice stop boiling. It will disrupt it. We want to keep the temperature nice and steady," he repeats.

I follow him over to the first blue fifty-gallon drum. He unties the butcher cord and lifts an edge of the polyethylene plastic so I can see inside. Curiously, it has the wet, black depth of Italian eyes but not so much, because there is pink foam and rigorous bubbling.

"It will go like this for a while and then when it is finished, it will stop," he says to me.

"I want to taste it," I say, genuinely interested.

"You can," he says.

"It is the only way to learn," I say teasing him and he winks.

The interior light in the garage makes everything gleam in a sort of sacred twilight. I feel like I am in Ali Baba's cave, surrounded by treasure and hidden from the outside. *Garibaldi* checks each fifty-gallon drum and then goes over to the workbench. He whistles quietly. I start whistling too, to see what it feels like. He has already entered the work-trance, inviting me in only when there is an obvious lesson to be learned. But I see a different lesson and it has to do with peace, and within that, the silence of being entirely who you are, where you are, usefully. Nothing more, nothing less. It is a good way to live. I can't help but wonder how he got this way. Questions begin to pool and then bubble up to the surface. Then they gleam. It is so easy to ferment around the old guy.

"*Nonno,* what was it like when you were a kid?" I ask him.

"*Eh?*" he says, and I repeat the question. He does this sometimes. He gives the impression that he has not heard you and wants you to repeat but I know that he heard me the first time, is translating and is now making the jump from *Inglese* to *Italiano* to memory. It is why I am always saying: *scusa? Scusa? Scusa?* when I am in the *piazza* in his Hometown. It is a good way to buy time. *Ripete per favore* also works well when you are in a pinch and know what you want to say but don't have all the words collected yet. It is … how you learn.

Garibaldi is searching, searching and then picks out a thought.

"We didn't have much to do with playing, when I was a kid" he starts off. "There was always the work to do, right from the time you were young. Even Carmine, when he was little and we were on the farm, his job was to feed the turkeys. When we got here, even when we would go for a walk, he would collect little twigs for the fire."

"What were some of your jobs?" I say.

"When I was a kid, about *sixseven* years old I had to look after the sheep," he begins.

"We didn't have too many, about ten. It was my job to take the sheep out to a little piece of land. One day, I sat down and I fell asleep. The sheep went wherever they wanted to. They ate a little bit here, a little bit there and then they went to another guy's land into his corn and into his beans. The way they went in there they destroyed everything with their feet. When they were full, they went back home by themselves. When they got back to the farm everybody wondered what happened. My uncle came out to see where I was, not because he was worried but because he figured I must have fallen asleep. When he saw the damage the sheep had done to the other guy's land he thought oh-oh there is going to be a lot of trouble. He let me sleep a little longer so he could walk around and take a look. But then he started to wake me up, nice at first.

" 'Angelo, Angelo, wake up.' he said.

" 'Angelo, Angelo, wake up!' "

"When I was wide awake he said to me, 'Where are the sheep?'

"I started to look around. 'Oh-Oh,' I said, 'they were here a moment ago. But that was an hour or so ago.'"

"That's when my uncle told me that the sheep were back at the farm. So we started walking and he was behind me. He got his belt off. I was wearing short pants, not like you have now. Mine were different, one had a leg up to here and the other leg was to my knee. All of a sudden, Bang! And I jumped!"

"Like a sheep!" I say.

"Yes like a sheep." He is laughing. "I jumped from here to here and then I started running but he was a young man, about *seventeeneighteen* and he caught up to me."

"Bang! Bang! Bang! All the way back to the farm. That was the punishment I got. The next morning my legs and my back were blue."

"Did your uncle tell your father?" I ask.

"No," he says. "I would have got it worse if he did."

"I disagree with that," I say and later we will argue again and again about how children must not be hit, but for now I ask, "What happened to the man who owned the land that the sheep trampled?"

"*Eh?*" he says. "Well, the owner, he didn't live there. It was one of his pieces of land but he lived far away. By the time he saw it, he must have figured out that somebody let the sheep run through there but nobody saw it so they couldn't do anything."

"How do you know he's still not looking for you?" I say, joking.

"I don't think he is there anymore. It was from a long time ago and he was my grandparent's age," *Garibaldi* replies, missing the joke, still off somewhere in the fields of Castropignano.

You can tell when he is back home. It is subtle but you can tell. With the men, it is not so much the eyes but the movements around the eyes, over the brow and in the outer corners, or maybe something in the cheeks, or the way the nose and mouth pick up when you are squinting through fog. His head moves slightly forward as if to see back in time and when he does that he is in the full flight of memory and I know there are pictures in his mind. Because I am enchanted, it is easy to follow him then, so I go.

We move over to the workbench. There are many hard, green tomatoes placed on top. By now, he has pulled the plants out of the garden and salvaged whatever he could before the frost stakes its claim. I see earthy onions and garlic in bushel baskets underneath. I smell their faint aroma. For now, however, the job is to tie up the green tomatoes and hang them in the *cantina* where they will ripen and when it is time—there is no rush—he will use them with satisfaction in the salad. It will be December and this will be the last bit of summer to reach the table.

I ask the question and he begins.

"When the war came, we had to leave the farm and move away to live on another little piece of land. The Germans came first. They took over our house on the farm. My father and I used to come back to our land and watch them from the corn. We had nothing to eat so each morning we had to sneak back to try and find something. After a while the Germans would let us come and we made them understand through signs that this was our house. They got used to us and every morning my father and I would go there. I was about *fourteenfifteen*. After a while it got dangerous to go. My father told me every time I heard an airplane to lie down on the ground. We were walking to the farm and all of a sudden I heard: *Rrrrrrrrrrrrrrrrrrrrr.*

" 'Get down, Get down!' I heard my father say."

"And all of a sudden, Bong! Bong!! Bong!!! Bombs were falling. I remember I looked up and saw a tree, this wide, get cut right in half," he says.

"So after that we had to be really careful. When the Germans had to go they always left one or two around to guard the back, I forget how you call it in English. One day my father was coming back from the farm and this German-guy yelled out for him to stop. He was pointing his rifle and my father started to run. The German-guy shot him in the leg and do you know my father was so wounded, he had to stay in bed for two years. Little pieces of bone kept coming out of his leg. The doctor left a little hole in his cast so he could pull them out. You see, my father had a long army coat on him that he got when he was in Spain. That made the German-guy think he was a soldier."

"How did Gino get to Spain?" I ask.

"It was Mussolini," *Garibaldi* says. "At that time, Mussolini wanted people to go to Ethiopia to live and my father wanted to go. He signed up for that but then Mussolini made a deal with Franco and my father had to go to Spain to fight in the war there. He was there *sixseven* months and never got a scratch. Then he came back to the farm and got shot."

"Was it hard to come to Canada?" I ask the old guy, keeping my questions short and clear. He is in full stride now and has woven a vine's worth of green tomatoes. He measures their weight, standing with an outstretched arm. They gleam in the twilight.

"When the war passed, we had nothing," he says, emphasizing the emptiness of his last word. "The land was ruined. There was no future. At first I wanted to go to Europe but we had nobody there to sponsor us. Adamo went to Argentina. So did Antonietta and Antonio.

They wanted me to come there. But Giovanni was already in Toronto, so he agreed to sponsor us and we came over. That was March, 1957," he says triumphantly.

"That was a good move," I say, sensing that the story is coming to a close. In the Court of *Garibaldi*, I, *Il Vagabondo*, the Italian night school drop-out, know that the Tales of *Gusto* and Enchantment have their own language, that they will ripen in the telling and the retelling like treasures on a vine.

"Did you know," I tell him, "that the very second you got off the boat on this continent, the moment, Lina stepped off the *SS Constitution* onto the docks of New York, on that fateful day, I was conceived and destined to meet Maria? The rest is, of course, now history."

"No, I didn't know that," *Garibaldi* says, creaking his way over to the garage door button. It rises in a slow resolute cranking letting in the grey, cold light.

"Open sesame," I say. Before I know it, the garage door is shut and we are inside the house washing up and getting warm.

Intervallo

*Il Vagabondo addresses his audience with things
that are important to know*

*(Eh, it depends how you like to read it, but there are a few things I
must tell you.)*

We get our veals from Commisso's on Eddystone, and our chicken
from Valencia at Jane and Sheppard. Go to Valencia before 5 p.m. if
you expect to get roasted potatoes. If you go after five p.m. you will
be crushed. There is no use. But if you go before 5 and ring the bell,
the woman will come out from the back. You will ask for a big, brown
whole chicken, turned on the rotisserie to perfection. They will put it
in a warming bag and price it. You will want two large containers of
roast potatoes in oil with rosemary. Look happy when they are
preparing them for you and they will put so many potatoes in that it
is hard to get the cardboard lids on. Do not buy your bread there.
Buy the sausage and the pizza. Now go to the meat counter and the
dairy section at the back. The *Asiago* is exceptional and the cold cuts,
not too bad. You are used to bologna or cooked ham, probably in
those convenient vacuum packages, so live it up, try the exotic cold
cuts and learn how to say them. Capicollo, Mortadella, Genoa salami,
picante, per favore, Calebrese salami and by now, if you have not had
prosciutto, you are a fool. Ask to see it first, nod like you know it is a
good one and ask them to trim the fat. They slice it thin so buy lots.
There is no point in tempting yourself if you buy anything less than
500 grams. Same with the Mortadella. Trust me on this. I can't tell
you how many times I came out of there thinking I had a feast, only
to be deceived. On the way back, you can go into La Stella to buy the

bread. It is not too busy and they will cut it for you. Check to see if they stock Rastrelli oil but they won't have it. Nobody does.

After that, maybe once every *sixseven* weeks, drive to Commisso's and go to the hot table. It doesn't matter when. Someone will be there all the time. It is open twenty-four hours a day, seven days a week. If you can go with your mother-in-law, it is better because they will see you with her and know immediately that you are *Inglese*; however, it will be a case of—how do we say it?—*paesano*-by-association. Later, when you go in there alone, you won't have to say three times that you don't want your veal on a bun. You want it in two tin-foil take-out containers, *quattro picante* with extra sauce and in the other, *quattro sweet* with extra sauce. Sweet (*dolce*) means not-spicy. Once they really know you, they will automatically add the hot pepper on top. You are coming out of there with eight veals. Get a small container of mushrooms in oil (*uno piccolo fungi*). For the rest, you are on your own. Go to the back and get the buns. They tell you to use the tongs but don't use the tongs because the tongs can't tell you if the buns are fresh. Just don't hesitate. Pick them up like you know what you are doing. Look like you are ready to yell back if anybody behind the counter says anything. They will leave you alone. The buns are good but it depends how you like them. La Stella can be your backup. On the way out, check for Rastrelli oil, but they won't have any either. If you eat the veal too often, they will lose their enchantment. Take them home and eat them immediately, like I say, once every *sixseven* weeks. Try to get some homemade red wine and Mio or pear juice for the kids. You are now fully prepared for the veal wars with your friends at work, who may be Italian. They think they know but they do not know. Everyone thinks their veal place is the best. It will get heated. If you want to win the debate, mention the calendars. The calendars at Commisso's are exquisite. In August there is Gitto di Bondone, the Resurrection of Lazarus, in January, Sassoferato, the Sleep of the Infant Jesus or in November, Caravaggio, the Rest on the Flight into Egypt. *Bella!* Now you will have names for your peppers when you skin them particularly skilfully in September. It is a gift.

Learn *scopa* quickly when you are indoors and *bocci* for when you are outside. *Bocci* can be played anywhere and it is fun to play it in between the trees at Wasaga Beach. After, when you are tired—

there is no rush—you will have a huge meal of lasagne or *penne rigate,* oil, vinegar and salt salad, prepared *al fresco* with as much cantaloupe or watermelon as you can eat. Try to play with a set of old rust-red and black stone balls with a white *ballino*. The plastic ones are tourist class.

Scopa is easier to learn then *Briscola*. Three cards, four in the middle, goes to eleven, it is not hard to learn the cards. *Il cavallo, la bella sette, the primiera* … once you know and if you are enchanted, you can go anywhere with your deck. Pride will swell your chest. Your children will teach it to their friends from Canada, Jamaica and Malaysia. If you lose the deck, or give it away, you can always buy a new one at any Italian bakery. If you are lucky enough to get invited to—how do you say it?—the Club, be prepared to lose a lot of quarters because the old guys are very good. They are so good they will invite you back to play. This is good because then when you see them at a *festa*, you can give them the hard time. You must get to the *festa*. There is so much food there. Too much food. Try the fish. There are many kinds. Thankfully, it is not a wedding so there will be no sweet table at midnight. Brandy goes good with *tartufo.*

I can see that it is time to go back to take our place in the Tales of *Gusto* and Enchantment. I am rushing now. I have taught you everything I know so you can get around in this new world and I will tell you one more thing: what you do at Christmas. Do not buy clothes for gifts. You will never see them worn. Do not go to Canadian Tire. Every tool you will ever need is in the garage, remember? Go to every used book store you can find and proceed directly to the Italian Canadian section. Try not to get the ones the modern guys write with the sex in them. The old guys don't really read that stuff. It makes them uncomfortable. What they really like is the stories about their immigrant experience: Zucchi, Gabori, Iacovetta. They are all beautifully written and will be highlights during the winter months in *Garibaldi's* Court, when there is not much to do and you are unable to go outside to work in the garden. They are things that Italian men absolutely don't need which is why they won't have them. You are smarter than you look.

(the lights are flashing and you may return to your seat)

Act IV

Scene 1.

La via Rita. Song of the Street

*The young guy and the old guy pass time
and survey the neighbourhood*

I am outside now on the clean cement hem of the driveway. *Garibaldi* is with me and we are passing time. It is such a curious thing because time performs differently on Rita Drive. It is first thing in the morning, mid-afternoon, early evening before supper or after supper when the light is softening. It could be any Saturday or Sunday or maybe even a weekday in the summer. It is cool and moist in the shade or the sun is beating strongly, pulsating bright white off the cement. It reminds me of the Hometown. The street lights wink and then they come on. People are going to church or people are getting married. They are dying. They are going to the store. They are walking up or down, this side or that. You can feel the threat of frost or the promise of spring in the air. Our part of the stage is just past the bend, same side as the church, six doors down. There is a procession and middle-aged men proudly hoist a saint up onto their shoulders. The sacred figure rocks mechanically back and forth but the people move fluidly and in colour. Their performance is enchanting. Encore! Encore!

I look left and see. *Allelulia.* I am inside St. Jane Frances Church this split second and it is eleven o'clock. I am getting married. Lamb of God, you take away the sins of the world, have mer-cy on me. There are forty or so *Inglese* on this side and thousands of Italians on that side. Mary has walked, with her bridesmaids, the six doors down to the Church. People stand in their own garages and on balconies to wave and to clap. Lamb of God, you take away the sins of the world, have mer-cy on me. Before God, *Ti amo amore.* There is an aisle and we walk as one down it, loved in chorus, this side and that. The doors burst open, like petals on a flower, and we are outside under the blue sky. Everyone spills out behind us into the sun. Lamb of God, you take away the sins of the world, grant us peace. The cars start their slow shuffle out of the lot. We sidestep them and walk the six doors up to the house, delighted. This memory is given to me every time I stand there. It is an eternal *bomboniera* from the neighbourhood.

"*Auguri.*"

"*Grazie, prego.*"

"Do you remember all the old guys looking at you at our reception line to see if you and Lina were happy?" I say to him out of the blue. "I think that once they knew you were okay, I was okay too, don't you agree?"

"Yes," he says simply.

"The sweet table was too much though," I tell him, our thoughts running vaguely parallel. It is before midnight and I send word to Rizzo's people not to make a fuss out of the mammoth table, tiered with sweets. I sense they are going to turn it into a spectacle. The music plays and the night sings triumphantly. Suddenly, the microphone cuts in, the music stops and our eyes are directed loudly to the beautiful table. I look to see who else is getting married but it is merely the food. It is—I don't know how you say it in *Italiano*—a *molto* extravaganza, or like I told you, too much of a muchness.

"You won't die from this," I am reminded while a breeze shifts my thoughts and for a curious second I chuckle, my shoulders sneer with the spice of cynicism.

"When it is time for church, you should sell parking spaces," I say to him.

Each Sunday Rita Drive becomes a tidal pool. The cars sweep in, the doors slam shut and some walk stately, others running lately, struggling through the undertow of time. Coats go on quickly over shoulders (sort of) and dresses are adjusted at the hips. The children are led, the young people aspire proudly to the grown-up world and there are always the self-conscious teenagers, still obedient enough to attend but on their own terms and in jeans, gold chains and track suits. It is *lecito*, permissible.

In an hour the tide goes out. I watch the procession, the good navigators and the ones who get it wrong time after time.

Never turn right and go up past the house or you will be trapped in the gridlock of purgatory. Sunday after Sunday, motion starts speeding up and for some reason, probably lunch, everyone is vaguely late and ever so slightly put-out. You can see people already starting their list for confession, the holy water still wet on their fingers, their snarling faces, the husbands in a frothy pantomime behind the windshield, the old women looking cold and bitchy, silently proud of their men, goddammit.

"You are smart to live so close and be able to walk to the church," I say to him.

"It was like that in our Hometown," he says back to me.

"Yes," I agree.

In this neighbourhood, whenever I drive up it is always like the first time I arrived. Via Rita is enchanted. Time here is slow and familiar. I stand on it while it shifts underneath me, around me, over me and within me. You can see everything that way.

"How do you ever get used to all these planes flying over?" I ask him once, in the early days. The Court *of Garibaldi* is right under the flight path to Toronto's International Airport. After all, it is North York. Any time you look up there are vapour trails scraping the sky. Like clockwork, every five minutes, the steel shapes descend over rebar string bean frames and shady grape vines. Once in a while you find yourself cursing the suspended animation of the plane. Tauntingly, it appears to pause directly over the house. It is deciding which path to take and then, suddenly, it cruises away much too low and much too loud.

"You get used to it," he says.

By the second barbecue on a Sunday afternoon, I am used to it. It is hot. My attention is completely focussed on the veal chops, smoking, sizzling brown and marinated in wine vinegar. They are heavily salted near the end and carefully stacked on the top grill when it is time to cook the sausages. Finally, when you taste the meat, the salt stings your lips. It lingers on fat-stained fingers. This pleasure is quickly followed by a lightly-oiled green salad, flecked with red radicchio, white onion crescents, wet tomatoes, quartered cucumber and more bitter red wine vinegar and salt. If there are green figs, you must eat six or seven of them.

It is a beautiful thing to stand there next to my old Italian guy. His street is before us. It goes up and it goes down and I never know why but it is time to wonder again.

"When we came here, there was not much north of Finch. First we lived on Montrose, in a single room rented by *Zio* John. He bought some furniture, a bed, and sent for us from Italy.

Then we lived on Blackthorn with *Zio* John. Joe and Pina, Domenico and Rosina lived beside us. Finally, we got our own house on Hope Street. We had someone stay with us, the lady who cleaned the church, to help us with the rent. We worked hard and when the house was ours we were happy. We knew that people were going to *JaneSheppard* and we decided to go when the houses were being built there. That was in 1973."

The key to talking to old guys is to learn to keep up with them. On the one hand, they walk so slowly and on the other hand they cover decades of memory in leaps and bounds. Try going around the block with them at 7 p.m. on a summer night when the light is softening and it is getting cool and not yet dark. It is the only time in your life where you will put your hands behind your back and rock slowly from side to side when you stroll. There is no rush. *Dio*, it is unbelievable. It is a—how do they say it again?—a *passeggiata*. Say it slowly. *Passeggiata*. It is such a beautiful word. *(See? You are passing time too. Bravo!)* When you make two right hand turns you are on a new side of the block. There is another row of houses on the other side of the street.

Take your time. You see wrought iron railing curling up magnificently around perfectly poured cement steps ascending to balconies. You first notice how clean the balconies look and that they are a mirror image to the one attached to the next house. You notice planter after planter of green leaves or red geraniums. The pots cascade down the steps naturally: big ones, small ones, plastic lions, ceramic bears. The lawn is small and inevitably, it is occupied by at least one fruit tree. It is blessed by a statue of the Virgin. All small rocks are painted white.

Flowers border everything. There may be a stand of ornamental mulberry trees or those beautiful ones with the broad, serrated leaves. I don't know how you call them, but you notice them immediately in the spring or the fall because they have been Italian-pruned, denuded so drastically you will marvel that they did not die. They should have died but somehow, I don't know how they know, but they know. I tell you this: it is one of the mysteries of *Garibaldi's* Court and it runs in the blood like the sap. My neighbours have stood around while Angelo and Mary prune our trees. You should see them, the disbelieving rabble, looking at one another, nodding their heads like they know. Some of the wittier ones bring by nursery flyers with the prices of the spruce, the maple and the mulberry trees circled. I collect the glasses when it is time to go in and a week later they beep their horns tauntingly. "*Vagabondo*, did your trees die yet?" Spring comes—there is no rush—and soon, the first green buds push off their husks and shoots come out and then new green branches and the leaves and when the children were little, our tongues. These pruners are legendary, I tell you, and the next year inevitably my neighbours politely ask, when is he coming up again?

The side yards have a row of more fruit trees planted in perspective. There are onions growing somewhere along the edge. You are able to make out two flags and because you are passing time, take bets. More often than not the Canadian flag is proudly on the top with the Italian green, white and red flying proudly, just underneath. Trust me on this and you will win most of the time in North York. It makes you feel proud and just a little envious. They know where they live, they know who they are, and they know where they come from. It is the sacred trinity of the second wave. I sometimes wonder if their children really understand it.

If the garage is open, someone will be inside. You nod and it is good to know how to say *buonasera, signore* or *buonasera, signora*. You can also just nod politely, as will they. You see the same things in *Garibaldi's* Court, but different. The fifty-gallon drum is black instead of blue, or maybe someone has a couple of the white ones that had lard in them, or vegetable oil. You wonder again where they got them. Depending on the season, you see the tomato apparatus, a bigger or smaller wine press, and different pots or pans, colanders or sieves.

Remember, everyone does it their own way. It depends how you like to do it. White-haired women shell beans; small, hard looking men braid garlic. If you are lucky and the sky begins to paint itself variegated red over thin wisps of dark cloud, you can see the husbands and the wives putting the garden to bed together. It is probably the most sensuous thing I have ever seen. Not sensuous the way the young guys write. Sensuousness, slightly out of view. Swaying to the rhythm of tasks to be done, in the proximity that love creates and gives away so easily. It is called "making a life" and when you see it, nothing else matters and you will want to make a life too. A hose is coiled up while the garden tools are collected. A pail is carried to the back while a rake is placed in the yard barn. Sheets come off the line while dry flower heads are pinched off. It is breathtaking. Like flames on a Castropignano hillside, you see scores of fields like this, patched side by side, and stitched gently by enchanted streets.

Slowly, you keep going, rocking this way and that. There is no need to talk, only to be or to see or to listen or to watch. There are children playing in the field beside the church and behind the school. Splashes of bright blue and yellow and orange shirts chase white and black checked balls. The priest's vegetable garden is now in shadow, but it is growing robustly so you know some old guy has swung by each morning to see to it. Make a third right turn now to pass the low-rises, the garbage dumpsters and the garish orange pizza shop, and by your fourth right turn you are back on busy Jane street heading north. You notice the litter and the cars, the neon "open" signs and all the street hubbub and you are starting to come out of the enchantment. *Garibaldi* pays no heed and keeps the same thoughtful gait. We round the gentle crescent, past the aluminium cross at the church, a silver blessing on the urban life, and return to the driveway at the front of *la casa Garibaldi. Bene, grazie.*

Yes, when you learn to walk slowly to keep up with the old guys you realize how quickly they tell their Tales of *Gusto* and Enchantment. How rich, ripe stories span decades of time in a moment. Slow down your mind—there is no rush. Be with them. Listen. Listen again. Each image, each word is a gateway to a new place. With a little practice, you will soon be able to speak their stories back to them in the dialect of love. They will *comprendi.*

It is not unlike being invited to walk out to one of their pieces of land. They want you to come, but be careful. It is not always easy. Go when you are not tired for the ground is uneven and the distance is tedious. When you finally get there and the old guys take you into one of their fields to pick the corn or to cut the hay, you will work hard, harder than you thought, for they have opinions.

"You are making the children nervous," he says to me one day. "He has to learn from his mistakes. If he falls, then he will know. *La planta si deve plegare quand'e tenera, che quando s'indurisce si rompe e no si piega.*"

"What does that mean?" I snap, missing the *lezione* entirely, the way quarrels push reason.

"We say, 'The plant you have to bend when it is tender because when it gets hard, it will break but it won't bend,'" he instructs.

"The children of today are not respectful!" he will accuse some other time, emphasizing the point, with his index finger. "If I talked to my father that way I would be hit. Bong, bong bong! Again and again and again."

And I admit there are *onetwo* times when I forget my place in *Garibaldi's* Court. There is no *gusto* in rancour. There is no enchantment to anger. There are times when old men must listen to young men. There are times when young men must listen to old men. It is usually the same time. The women do not like to see the men get this nervous and they will pat them on the shoulder and make "choo" sounds and say, "*Abbi pazienza, abbi pazienza.*" Enough. Have patience.

"You make me nervous," I say responding like a *testa dura*, a hard head. "Since I have known you, you have never once said, 'You are a good father' or 'You are a good man.' Never, not once. But," I say, rapping the table in dialect, "you are quick to correct me, to give me the *lezione.*"

I point my index finger directly at him now. "All this 'I don't know if I like you, I don't know if I don't like you,' it is nothing to me. Do you finally know today, tomorrow, next week? Did you know yesterday? How come you didn't tell me then? Did you forget?" And I smack the table with my open palm (translation: *I must teach you something now in hand dialect.* Smacking the table with your palm is different from smacking the table with your fist. When you smack the table with your fist to make a point it springs back up and usually, not always, the fist shakes and the index finger points for emphasis, suspended firmly in mid-air. This means you are in control and still capable of listening, perhaps readying yourself for your next point. But, when you smack the table with an open palm, palm down, this means that you are exasperated, that the conversation is over or "I disagree with you. Nothing you could possibly say now will convince me." This is followed by a sitting back action which is a signal that one if not both parties will stand up and end the conversation. I don't know how you do this in English. Everyone does it their own way.)

"The way I see it your father treated you kids like animals," I snarl, pressing out the anger with a solid pull on the bar, my hurt running out red onto the floor. "Gino was probably gentler to Rosie-the-Mule than he was to you and your sisters! Have you ever thought about that? When are you going to tell me when I do something right?"

"O-kay, O-kay, O-kay," he says holding out both hands over the table to gesture a sign of peace. I am sure if I sit closer he will grasp my hands and hold on to them.

It is the way it is with *Garibaldi*. It is the way it was with my father. Time creates a distance between ages and for a time, the translation of experience is lost. I see them weep. I see them explode. I see their humility when they adore *Jesu*. I see them be silly and tease their women. I see them kiss. I feel rough hands pull my neck down and scratchy beards against my cheeks. But still, between the young and the old, there are dialects of love that are different from one region to another. You can still be in Italy and not understand the fellow next to you. *No comprendi.*

No, you must even translate love in the enchanted place. I think I can. It is there slightly out of view, unspoken. It looks like a blessing on our marriage, a silent judge of character and a patriarch's leap of faith into God's Will. All the food I could ever eat; money if I need it; a place to stay; *pastina* for the *nipote*; a tool for work to be done, anything and everything, forever. It is that simple. It is—how do they say it—in their building? The Ministry of Presence. Put away your *Mondadori's Pocket Dictionary*, your *Berlitz Self Teacher*, your *Collins Gem*, your ES Teaching Cassettes, the Seeit&Sayit in Italian pocketbook that you keep in the car along with the CD for Dummies. Listen and find the common ground. It is always there. Sometimes there are no words. If you put your palms down and walk away you are a fool. Be smarter than you look.

There is any combination of struggle lying under the variegated shadows of anger. I have seen Italians hate Italians. On *via Rita* I heard that an Italian woman is beaten, slapped on the side of her head like a stupid dog. The wives know it and the men drink wine and laugh like they are your best friend. These are my friends and sometimes, they hurt themselves and each other. It is unfortunate. I hate it. I see Italians dead to other Italians. *Morte.* Old nervous women who will make a *problemo* anytime and anywhere. They are not right. They screech and all of it for what? For nothing. I too, have screeched in the Court. I pull an *Inglese* sword to defend my in-laws from the spirited onslaught of smug eaters-of-cake. *En garde.* And like I say, keep your palms up for when we learn to speak the dialects of love, we are all *paesani.* I don't know how you say it in English or Italian but that is the one thing that I do know.

The wind is out of both of our sails, like it should be by now. We are working too hard. It is time to quit and walk back from the fields.

"It is not that I think you are a bad father," he concludes sadly. I see a cloud pass over his face. "No, you are a good father. I don't tell you that because my father never said that to me. I am not used to it."

"You know that I respect you and that I love you, *Garibaldi,*"

"I know that," he says quietly.

"But you know," I say, a new breeze catching my sails, "I will be really sure that you love me if you let me take a big bottle of wine from the *cantina*, not those tiny ones you always give me. *Io sono Vagabondo! Grande vino, non piccolo vino. Dio, no, no!*" I say shrugging my shoulders, tilting my head, holding out my hands, palms up, for effect.

"I am out of wine," he says, cleverly.

On *la via Rita*, life changes and more stories spring, like songs from his heart. Before I know it, we walk all the way back to Blackthorn Street. I am not sure why, but it is to—how do you say it?—to retrieve something. A *lezione*, I think.

"It was about a few years after we arrived, that I got sick," he says looking at me seriously now. "It was the pneumonia. They say one of my lungs collapsed. For thirteen months I was there in the *ospedale*, in bed. My wife, she would come and see me with the kids. There was no one to look after them where we lived then. She would take the bus all the way. We had no money because I was not working. She had to go on the welfare.

"When I got out they gave me a huge jar full of the pills and told me to take them every day. I start taking them but after a while I say, to heck with it. I stopped taking them and I got better myself. We didn't have all that medicine in Italy," he says triumphantly.

Later he will get both of his hips replaced at St. Joseph *ospedale*. It is the time when the government didn't care about the people. There are cut-backs, and at night, there is no one in the hospital. It is urinous, like a Castropignano tomb.

"This premier is Il Duce," I will tell him and we will laugh.

During those long days of hip recovery, Lina will take a bus like it is nothing. She will go by herself and know how to get there. She will do that every night. She will get to know the bus driver. There is a cleaning lady down there who is a *paesana* and the women in the coffee shop, she knows. She will suffer but it is the way it is. She will not complain. She will not tell us how tired she is. She will not ask for a ride because she does not need a ride. She has created a system. It is efficient and she knows how it will go. When they first come to *la via Rita* and the children are older, she will work with some other women she knows at King and Spadina. She will sew clothes and take the bus home everyday. A new urban system. A quiet, determined pride, unspoken in *Garibaldi's* Court and because I can read the libretto, I can see it in my wife, too.

"We did not need the money," he will tell me on the steps underneath the peach tree, his pride slightly shaded. "But she wanted to go, so I let her go."

"It is good you let her go," I say in stilted English exchanging a very subtle, slight shrug.

"Yes," he admits.

"How come she never let me drive her to the hospital to see you?"

"When we need help, we ask for it."

The sun has come and gone. We can see the glowing interiors of cars driving by. It is mostly just shadows now. The yard barn is shut. The gate clangs and the latch is down. I trip the switch inside the garage, hesitate for effect and pretend to dive out of the way as the mechanical door comes down with a shuddering thump.

"Technology," I sneer.

I am in the car now. Wedged behind me, a large, old whiskey bottle filled with red wine, a white La Stella bag with a glass dish of *penne rigate* sits on the floor held tight by rubber bands. Next to it, another bag filled with bread and a third one with *bit a luce* for the children. Another day, perhaps it will be some zucchini or a new balsa basket of tomatoes and a bottle of wine or maybe even a clear plastic bag filled with soft green salad leaves, resting on a tray of figs.

We are between tides on the street tonight. It is not Sunday so I can go north. I sweep by Rocco's place three doors up, on the left. I see him in the shadow. He watches me pull out. So does Joe, four doors up on the same side as *Garibaldi*. I beep and wave now left, now right. All three of us laugh and I am home.

"I had a really good time today," I say to Mary.

"You always do," she replies. "Now what did Mamma send back with you?"

[Act IV]

Scene 2.

Lament: Come Back, Come Back to Rita

The street is changing

Franca and Luciano were the first to leave the street for Woodbridge. Rita was a branch then on a tall tree. When the two of them left, it was like a young sleek hawk pushing off. I felt the branch dip low, the leaves around it shiver and then the branch spring back, wobbling slightly in a rhythmic return to its place. Quietly, it changed tempo to join the gentle sway of a spring breeze. It was a motion that was somehow different. Different from the ancient *madonnas* creeping towards church. Different from the sons and daughters coming by for lunch on Sunday; their sleek, new cars pulling into clean driveways; the young bald men letting themselves go, their wives ever so slightly past bloom, the little ones spilling out of back doors slamming. Different from dark skinned, sinewy Orlando, in his sleeveless white T shirt, next door, ridding his truck of the bags of cement, rebar and a wheelbarrow for the garage. He comes home, set like concrete, every day I am there, in the evenings around 5:30. Different from the expectation of peach blossoms: we touch their twigs, inspect their buds and anticipate their annual promise from the juicy shade of the top step. And in a moment, a stutter, the misstep releases the vague premonition of unease. I feel it. We all do.

"Why is everybody going up to Woodbridge?" I ask *Garibaldi*.

"They are young, the houses are nice, they are going to make a life," he says in the practical cadence of the old.

"Wonder who's going to move in?" I say, following him to the backyard.

He is going to the makeshift greenhouse to check on his tomato seedlings. At the end of every May, I am in gracious receipt of two, sometimes three styrofoam flats of tomato plants for the garden. They are started in the garage, moved to the furnace room, transplanted to the greenhouse where the sun is warm and planted after the last frost. They are robust, like the people who grow them with sturdy, firm stems and good leaves. Plopped in the rich black dirt, you can jockey them around to fit in the trunk. They are tough and if a wine bottle falls onto them, it is not a problem, the stems won't break. If there is no styrofoam, a couple of wine crates lined with green garbage bags will do. As, I say, you can also use the wine crate for kindling, or perhaps, if you want to turn it up on its edge, you will see that it makes a fine table for the garden. You can set pots on it, or your coffee mug. I have seen wine crates used in garages as end tables to hold ashtrays. You can take out the bottoms and burn them, then use the frames in the garden if your soil is not so good. Fill the crates with rich earth and plant your carrots or your onions in it. *Perfetto*. We are still finding uses for them. It is the same with the purple *vin bon* twenty-litre pails. I will tell you the *segreto*. The Italiano twenty-litre pail, purple (you can get them in white) is the *Inglese* duct tape. It is true. You can tell who is Italian, or who is related to an Italian, or who is a friend of someone who is related to an Italian by the sheer quantity of purple pails on their property. For instance, if they are old friends of the family, the pails will be faded but there will be some new ones in the fall. If they are new friends of the family, they will only say they need one or two at first. However, once they become comfortable it will not be unusual to see ten or more pails on their property. We must have fifty. I never count. Some of them are very old and cut and scraped. Keep some up at the front of your house, the side yard or in the yard barn at the back. The obvious use is to collect the weeds or the grass clippings. Do not stop there. If you leave some in your garage, you can now wash your car. Watch out for the new construction guys though. They could care less. They will go into your garage and grab a pail or two to mix cement or paint, or grout. Why should you mind, you have so many. They will be careful to leave the dirty ones behind and it is not unusal to see a new one in their truck, filled with drills and hammers and screwdrivers. Why not? They know if you have sixty, you can get more. It is the way things are done. If you camp, you will need at least four. They are supreme end tables around the fire, waterproof storage containers or step ladders to put up your tarp. When your children are little, they will use them as drums, not snare drums, the entire kit—Philharmonic orchestra-grade drums. They are *professionale* after all and so are you. Save the white lids. You will never have as many lids as pails, so keep them safe. They have a black rubber gasket seal built right into the ridge underneath. Once you snap it on, it is a sure thing that nothing will get in or get out. They stack very nicely and high. I must warn you, if you do not look for the little white arrows on the lids and slowly, methodically open them like you are going around the face of a clock, you will skin your hand, pull back one or two nails and swear. It is guaranteed and useless to pull the damn things off any other way. Trust me on this.

We return to the driveway and Mary is there.

"*Buongiorno,*" we say, like strolling minstrels.

"Mamma needs you to go inside and pour more vinegar for the salad bottle," she says to her father in a voice that betrays its busyness. He goes in, looking happy that he has a new task.

"How come everyone is moving to Woodbridge?" I ask Mary.

"Because they are rich," she says matter-of-factly.

It is the church that changes next. The priest who married us is going to another parish.

We used to make a point of swimming through the current of people exiting the church, to go over to Father to shake his hand. He recognizes us and smiles slightly. I can tell he is glad that we are together. He tolerates that she is—how do the modern young devout call it?—a holiday Catholic and I, the *Inglese*, probably a good man who believes in *Jesu*. We go good together. He can see beyond. He can tell that we are making a life. I respect that and because I do, I am not condemned to enter his building every Sunday. I enter it freely, mostly during the Italian mass and at other times when I want to. It is part of how I make my life in *Garibaldi's* Court. It doesn't matter that I can't speak the language and I chose not to quibble with the ritual. I leave my judgement and I sing and smell and feel and believe.

It is an inner conversation that must be spoken and it translates beyond dialect into the life of the universal libretto of action-proper. It depends what you make of it, everyone does it their own way, but for me? It is the spiritual dialect of love that unites beyond words. It is—how do you say it?—my religion.

Still, the young people who show up Sunday after Sunday to perform in the electric band grow up. Their hair is shorter and a couple of them are starting to get plump. Periodically, new musicians arrive early to fill in the gaps and then, suddenly, all of the regulars are gone. It is our spirits that begin to fade first and then our bodies. Later that particular building will be practically dead to me when I go to one of the priests to ask him to minister to *Garibaldi* in his grief. He forgets to.

"Yes, yes, of course, I'll see him. Yes, Yes I know him. I know who he is."

"*Grazie, Padre.*"

One day, we see a "for sale" sign on Rocco's lawn and within a week another "for sale" sign across the road on Joe's property. They are going to the new houses up by Wonderland. There is a tree across the road, near Pasquale's that starts to die. This is an unusual thing to see in the midst of Italian men.

I see them cluster around a cherry tree, stake it, wrap it, put medicine on it and bring it back to life. I see them start new grafts and gently inspect their work in the morning. I see them pronounce a tree dead. Like checking its pulse, they pull out their knives and skin a little bark back to see if there is any green underneath, anywhere. I sense a bit of sadness, when all they see is brown. Quickly, the tree is taken out as a useless thing and resolutely they return from the nursery within a day or two to replace it. The new tree looks so fragile, like an immigrant at a bus stop. But it will be tended to, fussed over, inspected for insects, screened for rabbits and wrapped for winter. They grow things. It is what they do. It is who they are. I can see the fields in their eyes, the old hoes and their bent backs. My *contadini*. Sweat leaving clean trails on their arms. One or perhaps two donkeys piled with grain and ripe fig tree after fig tree shaking its fruit onto the ground, needing to be picked. Thin-necked jugs of water or wine hoisted in the shade. Minds emptied by tedium while the pile of corn that is husked grows taller than the warm green ones coming in from the field. At night we will dance. If one of these Italians ever moves next to you, you are lucky. *Garibaldi's* personality is more present in his yard than in his house. The yard is their living room and the living room is a place to go at Christmas. Their yard is their *al fresco* kitchen, an extension of the one inside the basement. And if you are beside them in August, remember what I said about the zucchinis.

Pasquale's tree is dead and it is still in the ground. It is over and I probably knew it before it happened.

Rita is a lament now. I don't see the sea of bodies carrying the crucifix up the street at Easter. Palm fronds are not fun anymore. We are not all coming out to the sidewalk on cold September days to wipe our grape-stained hands on rags. Fewer people wave now and there are more cars parked at the curb or tripled up in dirty driveways. There is more pizza trash, people change their oil on the street and useful things are thrown out. They sell Triple X movies on the corner now in North York and I haven't seen a Black Madonna for months. They pick out new trails to lead them to church. The Spanish fellow doesn't care that a case of *Carrignane* has gone up by a dollar and fifty cents, but I like the sound of his music. Across the street an enterprising Chinese couple convert their garage. They take the door clean off, seal up the space and convert it into a little factory. Why not? Everyone has to make a life. We trade hot peppers for spring rolls with the Vietnamese fellow beside us. He replaces Orlando and Maddalena. He consults with *Garibaldi* on the garden before it dies a little later on. The Jamaican house at the bend on the corner smells good.

What can I tell you? It wasn't always pretty. I know things that you know. You are smarter than you look and so am I. It is *la famiglia.* What do you expect? In these Tales of *Gusto* and Enchantment the demons on the street come back. So what? There are demons on every street. It is why we need the fire to burn off all of our stubble.

"One day," *Garibaldi* begins, "I was in the house and the doorbell rang. My wife she took the bus and the streetcar to St. Clair. She made a couple of sandwiches for me that I like. When I went to the door, there was an old Italian woman there. She put her fingers together and put them to her mouth like she needed food. *Ehh, ehhh,*

ehhh. What she really wanted was the money. I went to the kitchen and brought her back one of my sandwiches. She looked at me like I was a criminal. She took the sandwich but when I closed the door I said "To heck with you." In my Hometown, there was no money and if you were hungry you asked for food. To get some food you had to work for it. After that time, she never came to my house again, but walked up the street to go to the other houses."

"I see the *lezione*," I say to him and he nods.

I am standing on the upstairs balcony now, my arms on the cast-iron railing. Pasquale's tree is directly in front of me, it is cold and I watch the demons walk by. They march through my heart and I say goodbye to them.

I see an Italian fellow who was injured once, but he is okay now. He has been okay for years. He is not working. He does not want to work. His house is nice and the compensation is good. He is a strange, quiet fellow but his wife is so nice. Stumbling behind him is an old guy. They say he killed himself, I don't know why. There is a pair of Black Madonnas. They gave me tomatoes once when I helped them with their Valencia bags. Behind them are two women who make me nervous. One of them looks right up at me, suspiciously. Her eyes smoke, wondering the wrong things, and they no longer look like wells. The other is in pain and it is driving her to distraction. She yells at me for mysterious reasons. Bringing up the rear is the florid-faced fellow who drinks too much, and finally, that stupid, happy guy who beats his wife like a dog.

The procession fades.

[Act IV]

Scene 3.

Morte

The terrible grief

How can I tell you this again? We are one family. It is our turn to suffer. Did I tell you, it begins as two tiny lumps, about a quarter-inch wide, maybe a bit bigger? They walk in a little procession on the inside of her clavicle, nestled together, like twins. The silver chain of her crucifix is pushed by the crest of one into a little valley between the two. Yea, though we walk through those shadows, hoping against hope that it is just unbecoming carbuncles that old people get. It's not, and we know it. *Garibaldi* is not worried yet. The wife of *Garibaldi* shrugs her shoulders. She turns to the stove. The water boils and it is time to put the salt in and the *penne rigate.* Wherever her thoughts go, they go deep inside her and I see them fifty feet below in the pools of her eyes. She looks up and sees the moist concern in my eyes.

"*Panghe, panghe*" she says, pretending she is going to hit me with the wooden spoon.

"*Abbi pazienza, abbi pazienza!*" I say with a pretend scowl. I shake my left hand in a gesture that says, 'What am I going to do with you?"

"*Ehh,*" she says. Shrugged shoulders, cocked head, a thousand smiles wrinkling her eyes—it pushs the pain to the corners where a whirlpool of stirring takes it down.

I watch the ribbed *penne rigate* go round and round in the pot, pick one out and track it with my eyes. I see it dance on a hill of hot water and then it moves to the side and slips underneath. I lose sight of it.

146

Later when Mary and I hold on to each other and cry, when everything is lost and we know it, I realize that she didn't say "You won't die from this."

We are all dying now. *Garibaldi*, slowly, quietly, innocently. He appears vaguely oblivious to the whole thing. Carmine disappears into his own world to die silently, on his own. He will return as he always does, practically, when there is business to be done: accounts to settle, coffins to buy, a *paesano* to call about the flowers. Perhaps the pain is too great for them both. They run off, retreat to a little knoll to look back upon the nativity of their terminally ill, to watch and to weep. His stoic soul will rise to the occasion when the occasion calls hoarsely. Mary is dying so silently, so completely. She is within the friendship of her mother, as close as she can get into the little valley, fighting against all hope, fiercely trying to kill tiny cells one by malignant one. *Specialista* after *specialista*, one appointment at a time until there is no time.

"I cannot stand the *dottore*," I say angrily to Angelo one day. "He writes eternal prescriptions for pills that are killing her. It is in the papers now. Old women should not be taking estrogen pills forever. He should have reviewed her prescription years ago."

"It is not that," he says loyally.

It is years later when I finally excavate his reasoning. Perhaps it is a new story or an old story told from the next piece of land being worked. It depends how you look into the tale and from where it is told and when it last got interrupted. Stories are like digs. You get some pieces and some fragments and you lay them out, one by one on coarse white cloth. Some of the pieces have no meaning until you unearth another piece and put it beside the first one.

"In our Hometown," he says, "you had to send someone for the doctor. There were no phones like there are now. No, you had to go and find him and tell him what was wrong. When he came to your house, you had the hot water and the towels ready for him. He might leave a little medicine and tell you what to do. Back then, we had no money to pay him so if we had a little pig, we would grow it to be a big pig. We didn't keep the *prosciutto* for ourselves. We gave it to him. At Easter we would give him a bag of flour or some eggs. That is how it worked."

"Hmph. If you say so," I say, shrugging my shoulders.

In the end she has a—how do I call it?—a treatment. It is another little pill that gives us two more years in the valley. It is small and it is potent and it is taken daily. We will always be grateful for our last Christmas, the last time we are all together. The last time the cold, fresh air comes in the door and we stoop down and kiss her on both cheeks and pat her new hairdo to sidestep a smack. The coats are hung, the shoes and boots are taken to the furnace room to dry. Slippers adorn our feet and we time our last arrival, always just as the pasta is going in. The children check for presents upstairs in the living room and later, they find a rubber ball to bounce or to play catch with. A chair on wheels is turned into a gliding game on the painted grey cement floor by the laundry. Yells from the kitchen next door half-heartedly tell them to be careful. The children correctly translate, like they always do, that we are not getting up and they play even less carefully. I stir the boiling pasta beside her, slowly and lift the last lid of the *baccala* suspended in bubbling red sauce. It took me years to acquire the taste of cod in my sauce but I finally came around. Years later, I make it myself and it is not bad. In the oven there is battered cauliflower. I put out the crusty bread, the black and green olives, the celery and the *finocchio*. The nibbling begins.

The *cantina* is cool and the wine is at a perfect temperature, not too warm, slightly cold to the touch. I get the siphon going and return to the table. I endure the final *la tassa* and before we know it, we are rushing our coats on, quickly stepping into shoes to get to Italian mass, six doors down.

We go with *Garibaldi* who has already been there today, with her for morning mass. We join the throng of black leather jackets and tweed overcoats, the fur collars, jeans, gold chains and track suits. The light inside glows, the organist looks so beautiful and the smell of candles and incense lasts forever. Inevitably, the congregation starts to cough but the stained glass windows, the lights and the flowers on the chancel are breathtaking and distract. After a yuletide blessing, the throng sways out like bells ringing.

Outside, it is too cold to watch the cars go the wrong way. We play cards when we get back and at 10:30 there are the chestnuts and later the *panettone, torroni,* "S" biscuits or "I" biscuits, *caffè e espresso.*

148

At midnight we admire Rosie the Mule, standing vigil over *Jesu* with the camels and sheep at the base of the artificial tree bought in the 1960s. We exchange gifts and at around 2 a.m., we load the children into the car and call out *Buon Natale* into the cold dark night.

Less than two months later, I take her to Humber Regional Hospital on Church Street. She is barely able to walk and *Garibaldi* now understands what is happening. Already his eyes look far away. He tells no stories, he is no longer shepherd, and he allows the events to lead him. Everything must be said twice to him now.

"Daddy, I know you are listening," Mary will say exasperated.

Finally, an insensitive intern who I could murder with my bare hands and happily accept the final penalty, tells us bluntly that her kidney is dead. Turning, he abruptly walks away behind the doors that cowards go through when they give up the facts. She is kept for observation. Mary gathers up *Garibaldi*. I gather the coffee cups and the *scopa* cards, inspect the *bella sette* deeply and then swear. We drive to the dead home on Rita.

Sometime later we are back at the hospital, who cares when it was, and I have twenty minutes alone with my Italian, for me, just for me. My wise woman who knew my eyes and my soul and loved me for loving her daughter. *Ti amo.* I touch her cheek and stroke her silver hair. Our eyes share everything. We don't say a word but we know. Outside the relatives gather. The old Madonna *zias*, the brother, the sisters-in-law, the cousins, and the *nipote*, the grandchildren.

Finally, the nativity of death. *Presto. Morte.* Later I will wonder if they put up a poster in the Hometown but for now *Garibaldi* is ruined. Maria takes her pain deeply down into her eyes, it will come up again—there is no rush—and she holds her father.

"Daddy. Take Mamma's silver crucifix. It will help you."

He nods and she pours the chain into his hand.

Later, we will sit in the kitchen. He will be wearing the silver chain around his neck.

"She left me. This is all that I have of her…," he will say and start to cry.

There are hundreds of us at the mausoleum now standing beside the "apartments." It is just down the way from the Banquet Hall, off Albion

Road where we had our wedding reception and I cursed the sweet table. We watch the efficient internment, the *click-clack, click-clack, click-clack* of the caulking gun. The creamy seam is smoothed beautifully with the putty knife, the facing placed gently on and screwed in with the bronze fixtures. Quietly, the two men gather up their tools to disappear around the corner. We are alone. Scores of flowers rot outside at the entrance and we return to North York.

Act V

[Act V]

Scene 1.

Death of a Garden

The old guy and the young guy mourn together
and tell a few more stories

About a month later *Garibaldi* almost burns down his Court. Lost in his grief, he has taken to placing a memorial candle in a pot of sand. Somehow, he falls asleep, it tips over, something catches fire and he extinguishes it. Fittingly, there is black ash residue all over the downstairs kitchen, the little TV area, the furnace and laundry room, the stairs leading to upstairs. It is like a shroud over the happiest places in the house. We do what needs to be done. We clean it, spotless, the way she would have cleaned it.

"She was my guide, my companion," he will say over and over again. He will throw his hands up in the air, clap them, and then shake them clasped before his heart. The patriarch has fallen. Nothing holds his interest. The days are hard but it is at night that he suffers, suffocating, crushed by three hands of a clock that circle without meaning.

The last time Mary is down with him, I hear that he has been singing. He is singing and then he cries. He cries and for a tiny moment there is a little peace, like the space in time before the next wave crashes in. Like a piece of driftwood, I arrive after work the next day. *Il Vaga-bondo.* He never knows when he will see me or where I will wash up. I have a better chance at finding some food that way. Otherwise, he will hide it. And the wine too. He lets me in but he looks older now. The old joke isn't as funny. I take off my shoes and follow his heavy shuffle into the kitchen. There is dust along the edges of the baseboard and some old spill splotches crossing the threshold in a tell-tale dribble. It startles like a slap in the face. She would never let the house get this way. It would be a capital offence, a violation of Rule G. To me, the house isn't really all that dirty but any dirt and dribbles stand in stark contrast to the way it used to be.

Underneath the stairs leading to the top floor is a tiny crawlspace with a small door. You must move the garbage pail, open the door with a decided pull and bend down to get in. It is easier if you just give in and go down on all fours. It is a woman's space. The first thing you see is two or three white Raggedy Ann mop heads slouched on nails driven into the stair steps, a new, slim wooden pole and extra bags of clean yellow sponges that slide into the slots on the base of the handle. There are extra green rubber gloves, at least one never-used pail, and jug after jug of bleach.

"She is always stocking up," Mary says.

Economy-size boxes of laundry soap, unopened bars of Sunlight soap and at parade rest, glistening green bottles of dish detergent, commanded by at least five new orange plastic bottles of Ceramica Bella. *Attenzione!* Do not be fooled by imitations.

"Every Saturday I had to get up early and help Mamma with the cleaning," Mary will tell me with open contempt. "There was dusting and vacuuming upstairs, laundry to do and to fold, fresh sheets to put on the bed, sweeping and mopping the downstairs floor. My brother was always in his room, sleeping in. They would not think to ask him to clean on Saturday mornings," she adds, bridling at the injustice but resigned to the fact that "that was the way we did it."

"I don't know if it is good to be so clean or it isn't," I used to think to myself until I did some more excavation, pieced together some additional stories and held the fragments up to the light. Like I say, *lezione* are like artefacts. When you see them, you see them. We are smarter than we look.

"Back then," *Garibaldi* says, "the house was not like we have it now. There were no floors like we have now. There were clay bricks, maybe one or two chairs and a big table by the fire. The fire was where we cooked and how we kept warm. Underneath were the stalls where we kept Rosie and the pigs and the sheep. That was all we had."

We found the last envelope with two hundred dollars in that little crawlspace, while we were down on all fours. We shifted a bleach bottle and there it was. After she died we found envelopes in the laundry room, in a pot in the back *cantina*, underneath the sheets in the linen closet upstairs, on the top shelf of a kitchen cupboard behind a cup. You never know what life might bring. If you didn't work hard you would suffer more. Waste nothing. Save everything. Be prepared in case trouble comes to you.

"I understand why Lina stocked up all the time," I say to *Garibaldi* one day when he is happier.

"You are learning," he says.

But she is dead and we are in the kitchen. I take my place across from him.

"Did you drink all the wine or did you pour it down the sink when you saw it was me?" I accuse him, after noticing the empty Alberta whiskey bottle on the white saucer.

He barely squeezes out a smile and motions with his head in the direction of the *cantina*.

"What are you eating? Is there any left?" I say upon return.

By now, his mood passes across his face and I see that he is coming out of his grave.

"You arrived too early," he says with a mock crestfallen shrug. "There is still some food."

Even when you are sad, I have to tell you that *gusto* is in the simplest of tastes. Don't ask me how he makes it; I still cannot get it right. On the counter is a bowl with some potatoes in oil. Boil the potatoes and when they are cooked but still firm, drain them and let them cool. Add some oil, not too much oil, Rastrelli if you can find it, but Colavita will work. Maybe press some garlic and mix it all together. Cut up hot pepper rings and add a tiny bit of wine vinegar. Serve immediately with crusty bread and *picante*, store-bought Molisano sausages preserved in oil. Remember what I said. Once you pry the first one out with two tines of your fork, the rest will come easy. You may wish to open a can of green peas and warm them lightly in oil. Add some onion. It is helpful if you are not wearing your work clothes when you eat this. If you are thinking clearly, you will save the leftover oil from your store-bought Molisano sausages. Good for you.

Now take some dried red peppers from the garden, slice them up and let them steep in the oil. It depends how you like to do it, but the more peppers you put in and the longer you let it sit, the hotter it will get. Dip only the tines of your fork into the hot mixture, and let it drip onto your potatoes. Repeat *threefour* times if you are crazy.

Many of my Italian family, or at least the ones that haven't died on me, are Molisano. It is the way they taught me. It is the way I teach you.

We hold hands across the table. I notice that he has not shaved today. We recite the Italian prayer. We say nothing when our glasses clink. It is obvious who we are toasting. Too obvious and I break the silence.

"Mary tells me that you are singing now." ("I've got an idea for Daddy," she tells me one night.)

"Yes," he says.

"Did you know that you used to sing all the time when you were working in the fields?" I say, giving him a *lezione*. "It helped you to pass time and it made you happy," I add, goading his memory. "It was—how do I say it?—*la vita opera!* The opera of life!"

He smiles his assent. He loves me (*shrug shoulders here*). It doesn't matter that I butcher the language and turn the libretto into *dolce inglese* sausage.

"Well then I have something for you. And you must take it. Maybe one day you will let me hear you."

It is a piece of the technology. This man can take apart and fix a furnace motor, design a brand new piece for the grape crusher, pinch off the copper end of a pipe and attach it to his hose to get an absolutely perfect flow of water onto tomato plants, but you should definitely go slow with them when you are explaining how a micro tape recorder works and especially how to change the tape and talk into it. Naturally, he catches on.

He is a minstrel. I am still humming his beautiful grief songs. They sound just like the Alan Lomax recordings of *Abruzzi,* moving in time as the sun comes around the back and you have all the red peppers you can peel.

Later he will need something else to occupy him. Mary is worried.

"I have two more ideas," I say, taking my turn.

"Angelo, you are getting too good at this technology," I tell him one evening. "I have something new for you that will simply amaze you. It is unbelievable. You will wonder how it is possible that you did not think of it before. You will offer me wine after I tell you so I don't have to steal it from you anymore like a *Vagabondi*. Soon there will be food in this house. Always! But..." I say, holding up a finger ...

He is listening now and enjoys the game.

"... A computer! *Eh!* What do I need a computer for?" he says, interrupting my speech. He is smiling doubtful little smiles and he raises his eyebrows at me. He shakes his hand in subtle circles as if to say, "My son-in-law, at first I didn't know if I liked you. Now I know I don't like you."

"Trust me on this," I tell him matter-of-factly. "In your stories you tell me you are a peasant, a farmer, so poor. But this is not true. I think you lived in town as an *artisan*. You are—how do I express myself in your language, it is so difficult?—you are—*come si dice?*—*artistico*? Yes, you are a poet. You sing beautiful songs. It is time that you write now. This is your *lezione. Abbi pazienza. Dio!*"

Thankfully, Mary has found a machine that is like the Rambler he worked on in the 60s. You can get under the hood and fix it with a long, homemade screw driver if the engine breaks down. I show him how to re-boot it on the back with a little paper clip. For a minute, I think he wants to take it apart to study it.

"This is not for taking apart," I say to him with authority. "It is to write with. It is better than a typewriter. It will help you with your grief. Write stories or songs or poems or whatever you want. You will never know when I will reappear to hear them or to bring back my empty bottle."

Soon Mary has taught him how to use the word processor, how to save files, how to print. His large, thick fingers spring over the keys with a sort of bemused gaiety. We have won another round against his depression. Soon—there is no rush—his work begins to appear at the mausoleum (*the apartmento*) taped to her granite plate on the wall. We are so tired.

Perdendo La Sposa
Da Angelo Molinaro*

Piangio di giorno
Piangio di notte
Piangio di mattina

Piangi di sera
Perche mi trovo
nella dispara.

Giacche'il buon dio,
si ha preso la mia consorte,
questa sara'la mia sorte
fino alla mia morte.

*shared with kind *permesso*

"It is *my* Solitude. *My* Depression," he tells me again, one day after work. "I am not living my life now."

He is not really going to the Club anymore. All the men have to leave at 3 p.m. anyway to pick up their little *nipoti* from school. Resolutely, proudly they get up to go. Metal chairs slide back. They have a purpose. They are rich men. It is obvious they are content and in love. It so sweet to see them wobbling home to *Nonna* with their little ones or patiently waiting in the park for the mishmash scooting lambs to stop, and return to make their giggling declaration: "He is my *Nonno*!"

Late afternoon is *Nonni time. Nonna* may be resting before supper or maybe she is at the stove warming up a little *pollo zuppa*, with soft orange carrots and little pasta stars swimming in it and a little cheese sprinkled on top. Perhaps she is watching Italian TV. *La Farfalla* (The Butterfly). She is so warm and cozy. It is a time for hanging up coats, the quiet transfer from *Nonno-in-the-parka* to *Nonna-with-a-little-bottle-of-juice*. The Divine Day Care of North York.

"Nico, Daddy's here. Go to the furnace and get your boots. It is time to go home now," I hear her tell Nicholas one day, completely in

Italian, when he is about two and a half years old. To my utter amazement, he completely understands her, fetches his boots, and comes to the door by the *cantina* to give me a hug. He is smarter than I look.

"It is time to go now, Daddy" he will say. I will pick him up and we will kiss her on both cheeks. He will clutch a little bag of roasted almonds for the drive home.

No, *Garibaldi* is not really interested in the Club anymore. He is no longer interested in the *festas*, either. There is no one to go with him. I see old men come up and grasp his arms. They say nothing. They look at one another directly and he will cry a little bit. They look sad, and then part. Tender old women will bring him a little pasta or a little sauce and some sausages or lasagne. He will try a little but most of it will sit starkly and foreign-looking, out of place, like boarders in a bare fridge. It will be offered to me or thrown out eventually. Like everything else, there is no heart or soul in the downstairs kitchen anymore. That living stage is just a place now, to sit and listen to bulbs hum or to clocks tick. There is really nothing to do but drink wine, sleep forever on your arm, let the candle burn down, wake up suddenly, fall and bang your head.

The telephone rings at 11 p.m. He has hit his head again and this time he is at Humber Regional. I will retrieve him, bring him back to his Court and then sleep over.

Mary and I begin to think about the retirement home. It depends how you do it but for me it is like putting the cat in a cage. He is an outside creature and would not feel comfortable indoors. Maybe I am wrong but there is no *cantina*. No garden. No garage. Nothing to fix.

We talk him into getting a cleaning lady once every two weeks. Rosaria will come and approximate a life. He will have someone to talk to, someone to visit him and his home will be clean. A nurse will periodically visit him and he will enjoy the company but it is clearly not enough. His solitude is causing time to blend into one long wall that runs the length of his life. There is really no morning or afternoon or evening or weekend. Just a wall of time.

We are outside now. It is dark and I am about to leave.

"Angelo," I say in a variation on the old joke, "do you think it would be a good idea if I take a bottle of wine up to Bolton to see if it tastes as good up there as it does down here? It is an *importante experimento* that I think I should try, but I need to know your opinion."

"I know you think it is a better idea than I do!" he will say.

His humour is back and I have sprung my last good idea on him over dinner and another tiny enchantment. Veal cubed very small. Heat some oil in a pan. Add garlic and some little onion crescents and finely chopped pieces of red pepper. Sprinkle in the veal and brown it nicely. You should salt it a little bit if you like salt. I do. When the veal is ready add a can of green peas. Stir gently and heat. Spoon into two bowls. Put out some crusty bread. Peel off the purple wax edges of the *Asiago* cheese that you have already brought to room temperature. The really good *Asiago* will be dry and will crumble or break even though you try to cut it uniformly with a knife. I may have told you this already. The useless *Asiago* cheese will cut smoothly. Do not buy this type. It is troublesome and I still don't get it right sometimes. She always did. Go to the *cantina* and get the wine, two glasses, the Mio glass is for you. If you are lucky, one of the women from across the road will have dropped by during the day. You may find some roasted eggplant or for dessert, some sugared orange peel. I have not been to Sugared Orange Peel School yet so I cannot advise you. I am not sure if I like it, I am not sure if I don't like it. It is how you should feel when you first try either *Brio* pop or store-bought *torroni.*

One day, Mary and I pull into the clean driveway on Rita. There on the boulevard is a large brown steamer trunk. It is weatherworn with wooden slats and solid hinges. It sits beside the recycle container and the garbage can.

"Mary," I say, "tell me they are not throwing that trunk out. Tell me that that is not the trunk that came over with you on the *S.S. Constitution.* What are they thinking?"

"Ma, why are you throwing out the trunk?" she says, kissing her mother on both cheeks.

"*Eh*, we don't need it anymore," she says simply.

"*Panghe, Panghe!*" I say, gesturing a slashing motion in the air with my right hand. I stoop to kiss her twice.

Garibaldi is in the garage fixing something.

"Angelo. It is—how should I say it?—*incredibile* that you are throwing out such an important part of your family history. How can this be? Why are you throwing the trunk out? This is not right," I say to him at the back of the garage by the workbench.

"We don't need that anymore," he says in his sing-song voice. He is whistling happily aimless notes, the afterthought cadence of the concentration of repair.

"I am going to save the trunk," I say to him definitively.

"If you want to save it, you save it," he says breaking the tune and then returning to it.

I go to the boulevard, inspect the steamer trunk, run my hands along the top over the smooth wooden ribs, open the hasp and the lid, inspect the slightly ripped, light brown interior, sniff for mould, close the lid and the hasp and gently place it, like Moses' basket into the back of our car. I notice a broad iron pan wedged in the top of the garbage can. It looks ancient. For some reason I have not seen it before. Perhaps it was tucked under the work bench, a Hometown nest for nails or screws, nuts and bolts. The word "antique" is *Inglese* and does not apply to what I see. What I see is an artefact, it is—how shall I put it—"of the life." I rescue that as well.

Maybe it is because so many of my childhood toys found their way to the white elephant sales at our school, or so many of my father's tie clips and cufflinks, my mother's costume jewellery were lined up for five cents, ten cents on portable tables in the gymnasiums of my Hometown, but for some reason, I am enormously sad, almost frightened, and I know that the treasures of the second wave of Italians are slowly finding themselves in garbage cans or, for sale, on sheets and little tables at yard sales all over North York. The treasures are melting like the once proud *Castillo* of Castropignano, back into the rock that they came from. It is a huge loss to see that story and those artefacts melt into nothing. At least I can rescue two things. And before I leave, I also rescue the coarse white *telio*-made sheet that is draped on the van seat in the garage. Later, when *Garibaldi* actually does *comprendi*, he will pull out a small blue and white metal ladle that came over in the trunk with them. He understands the lesson.

"There used to be a metal handle that went from here over to here on this pan," he demonstrates for me inside the house. "We cooked everything on the fire and with that piece you could hang it. There was a little hook that came out of the wall. I don't know where the hanger is now. We used this to make *polenta* or to cook the vegetables in, like a stew.

"Why did you pack it? There was so little room in the trunk."

"At that time," he says, "when we came over, we didn't know what we would find. We had to eat so we brought it. We took the plates and the cups. Everything was packed tight-like. We used the sheets to cushion it. The sheets were for the bed."

"Don't you see that we have to save this stuff for the kids? It is part of their heritage," I say seriously.

"Maybe," he says and I can tell he is fitting the idea into his mind and liking the feel of it.

Later, we will all pile onto the train and head to Hull to see *La Presenza* at the Museum of Civilization. Maria, *Garibaldi*, the kids and I will cram into a hotel room across from the exhibit. We will pick up thin red wine at the corner *dépanneur* and we will find a place to sit in our room to talk and share the day. He is silhouetted against the fading light in the window. He is happy. I am happy. We have seen the old photographs of pigs about to be slaughtered; men and women in the fields; the interactive exhibits on how to make a bread, or pasta. We admired the old tools hanging everywhere. *Garibaldi* is our tour guide, miming for us with the sickle, the scythe, telling us how they were used on his piece of land. For a time he leaves his world of grief and he takes us back home with him. On the return, I gaze from across the aisle at the four of them happily with one another: Maria leaning into her father; *Garibaldi* watching the kids engaged in the endless elbow wars for the armrest in the middle. The soft enchanted lamplight of night on a train. Maybe they will say something. Maybe they won't. It is the quiet time after an adventure when you are happy and let what you saw mingle with ripe thoughts of going home. As they become restless, the *scopa* cards come out and I will trade places with Maria. My *bella setta*.

"She was my guide and my companion," he will say over and over across from me at the kitchen table. I will hold his hand and love him.

"You and Maria, you have done a lot for me but there are some things you cannot do. It is my solitude. My depression. What I need is someone to be with, who can cook for me and clean my house. I need a guide. I need a companion, not a companion of the bed, but a companion of the life. Who can give me that?" he says helplessly, throwing up his arms and clasping his hands together with another slap. It is a hard thing to see.

I am afraid that his depression is winning. It is spring and his garden is a wreck. It is dead to him. The first thing you notice is the weeds. They are obscene. Next, you see that the ground has not been tilled. It is hard and unyielding, unhappy, not germinating, devoid of all life, bugless, dry. There are no bees. Behind him, Vincenzo's garden is living. He plants his tomatoes and stakes them enormously high in anticipation of their bursting forth. His bean house is newly rebarred. It is the same with Maddalena's and Orlando's and with the fellow two doors down; I forget his name, who grew the giant zucchini that embraced us all in such a joyous hug. I stand at the exact place, years ago, where I sat and passed time with Mary. The Court of *Garibaldi* lies in ruin. There are a few flowers left in the side garden, perennials, popping up despite the pain. I do not yet see the metaphor in their tenacious growth. I survey death. For Christ's sake, I am weeping and so is Maria. What do you expect? Death turns life into meaningless space and time and place and when that happens it is easy to be bitter. It comforts me. We aren't getting any stupid tomato plants this year. I will grow my own and bring him some. It shouldn't be that way, but it is. We should have had at least two barbecues by now. I haven't had the good sausages from Eddystone Meats since she died. What can I tell you and I don't care if you shrug your shoulders here or not.

"Angelo. I have more than one piece of land to take care of. You know that. It is so far to get to them all and sometimes I have to walk for hours. At night, I build a little house with corn stalks and Maria and I and the kids, we sleep in it. The next day we get up with the sun and work. You know, it is the life. But we are happy. I have a little piece of land in your garden now but I cannot get there every day. I need you to keep it for me. A few tomatoes, some hot peppers, some *cipola* and that soft green lettuce you grow. I have no money to pay you but I have something to trade," I tell him desperately over mortadella sandwiches and *Saputo provolone* cheese on crusty Italian bread. There are no olives.

He is listening.

"You and I, we should make a book!" I say to him, smacking the table with my fist and raising my index finger. That is what I will trade. "We could call it The Things They Carried: An Italian Treasury. It could be like a—how do you say it?—like a coffee-table book. There could be a chapter for everything that people brought with them to Canada. There could be a little map in the front of Molise province with Castropignano and all the other Hometowns marked; Torello del Sanio, Oratino, Montagan, Petrella, Sant'Angelo. Next to that could be a map of North York. We could set up two advisory groups: the old guys and the young guys. The old guys could share their memories and tell us what everything is; the young guys, maybe some girls, could do all the running around and design the book to get it ready. It would be a gift to everyone from Molisano. The *nonni* would like it and their children would have to have it. We could make it a universal book. We could put recipes in it, and every chapter could have sayings like 'When you move the compost, it will stink.' We are going to need a place to store all the artefacts and photograph them. We could get Johnny Caperchione to help us. He knows everyone and Mario is *presidente* of the Castropignano Club. I am sure that he and Nicolina would help us if you ask him to. I am going to email some people at the University of Toronto, Italian Studies program. Maybe they could help us. Who cares if they don't? What do you say?"

"Maybe," he says, shrugging his shoulders.

Scene 2.

March of the Grafted Limbs.

Garibaldi searches for a guide and a companion.
The journey to El Dorado

"It is not possible," I tell him, my wide eyes following the line of my finger to the tree. "You are a—what do we call it?—a *mago*, a sorcerer."

"It is possible," he says with a delighted grin. "I will show you how it works."

He takes me over to the plum tree and I inspect the phantom limb. It looks luminescent, ethereal, back-lit by a breeze gently stirring the white fluttering undersides of leaves.

"Look," he says.

It is the beginning of a *lezione* in *Garibaldi's* Court. The enchantment of Italian thought. Remember what I told you. First you must see the thing. Gaze at it. Look underneath or from the top or, now, facing the garden. You must inspect it. Once you inspect it, you touch it with your fingers, once, maybe twice. Now that you have touched it, you get it into your mind. Here, you can turn it over and over inside your head like you are already at the work bench in the garage. Hold it up to your light and say "holy mackerel." Turn it, see the problem and call on other thoughts to share their experience of your past solutions. You are—how do we say it?—you are consulting the problem. What tools will you need? Who could do this back home? Did you see someone do it at the old place on Blackthorn Ave.? No, you don't think so. But you have an idea of how the thing works now and once you have that idea you are ready to begin. Go to the garage and get your tools—everything you will need. Start to whistle. You are concentrating and not quite present to anyone, vaguely aware of your surroundings. There is nothing else to do right now, but this. Try your first idea. If that doesn't work, try your second. Stay with it until you get it and when you get it, stand back and inspect it. Inspect it again. The light is changing now. It is time to gather up your tools and bring them back to the work bench. With a cloth, you will clean them and put them back exactly where they belong. Trip the switch and as the garage door jerks down bumping shut—there is no rush— your song is finished. You will know it is time to go to the utility sink in the furnace room, wash up and have a glass of wine. It is the education of the life and you are the student and the professor all at once. What doesn't work is merely the early stage of what will work later. *Abbi pazienza.* Eureka! *Chin chin.*

"First, you make three cuts like this," he says. *Garibaldi* is holding a branch in his left and pretending to snip open the skin of the bark with the index finger of his right hand.

I see how you peel the bark of the plum tree ever so gently, not too much.

"Then you take a little piece of *albicocco*, a twig. It must be young and tender. You put it like this and then you wrap it up with the string, nice and tight. It doesn't always take, but sometimes it does. When it does, you have a branch like this one with *albicocca* and all the rest are the plums. That … is how we do it," he says, triumphantly and with a grin.

"It is brilliant," I say. "*Garibaldi.* You remind me of a young me!" Later, at the new house, I will see him be a *mago* again, but curiously, the graft does not take. The magic is not as strong there. We are some-how a little happy about that. It is unbecoming.

He finishes the lesson now. Apparently, you can do this with a plum and an apricot but you can't do it with a plum and a peach or a peach and an apricot.

"Why not?" I say, genuinely interested.

"It is because of the bone," he says. The plum and the *albicocca*, they have a similar bone inside. It is smooth. The bone of the peach, it is different, it is—I don't know how you say that in your language—it is…"

"Wrinkled?" I offer.

"Yes, wrinkled."

He does not know it, but he traded me a word. To this day I never refer to peach pits as pits, only as bones. The wasps in *Garibaldi's* Court pollinate everything when they are not singing *Dino Martinelli*. It is a gift.

I begin to notice that there is more talk about the sisters. They are Giulia and Caterina. Giulia is across the road, beside Pasquale. She was married to a Russian fellow, Piotr. He was always so tall and so friendly. If you saw him and didn't wave you are a *buffone*, a fool. I believe he took an interest in Angelo's half-children coming to see him on Rita. Giulia is coming across the road a little more too. Caterina? She lives over by Finch. One day, I will go over with *Garibaldi*, early in the morning and I will help with the sauce. It is here that I learn that you throw a potato in the huge boiling pot when you seal the jars. (*I told you. It is your clock.*) When the potato is soft, it is time to pull the jars. It depends how you like to do it. That is how I do it.

"You take such an interest in these things. It is unusual. Have some more," Caterina will say to me at lunch (*pranzo*). The conversation will pause and they will look surprised to hear any *Inglese* spoken at all. They will look at me like I am here for the first time, at the table and then the laughter and the happy cadence will resume. It is an international phenomenon.

I am eating thickly cut pieces of wonderfully hard *prosciutto*, *calabrese* salàmi, *piccante e sweet*, Friulano cheese ("Take as much as you want") and a different kind of bread that I am not used to. I'll get used to it, along with the homemade wine, so different from *Garibaldi's* but strong enough to invite you to a nap in the afternoon. There are black olives and sardines, salty rewards and part of the trinity of a morning's work in the backyard. The food is good, the work is hard and the company, merry. It is that simple. What else do you need? (*shrug shoulders here.*)

"Giulia seems nice," I say to him one evening after work. I heat up five or six of the frozen veals she brought over to his fridge. They are so easy. Pry them apart from the stack in the freezer. Heat some oil in a pan, less than five minutes a side, pat the excess oil off with a paper towel, repeat to infinity, serve with bread.

"She does not want to live in this house," *Garibaldi* says to me. "And I do not want to move."

He catches my interest and I stop patting the veals, pour some wine in his glass and mine and go to sit opposite him.

"It is not like I don't miss her," he says to me. "I miss her. So much."

He claps his hands in the air here but it does not have that desperate quality to it. He is not lost. He is working on the problem, inspecting it. He is fixing something. I am silent now, listening.

"At night, my solitude suffocates me. When I went to the *festa*, the sisters brought me up from my Depression. I was happy again. I was happy," he repeats breathlessly.

I start to cry a little bit around the eyes but, what the hell, I don't care, it is the way it has become in *Garibaldi's* Court and I am a rich man.

"She was my guide and my companion but I don't have my life anymore. I do not know how long it will be before I will die."

"You know I love you and I will do whatever you need me to do," I tell him.

"Yes, I know that," he says. "I think you are this way with me because you miss your father," he says, out of the blue … like he can see deeply into wells, the way I can.

"I don't believe it. He is not only a poet but a social worker as well," I tell Mary, that night. I am surprised, exasperated, and I feel completely understood.

"How does it feel?" she laughs and gives me a hug.

"What I need is a companion," he repeats. "Someone who will cook for me, and clean my house and help me. Not a companion of the bed, but a companion of the life," he says seriously, like he is saying it for the first time the way old men do while forgetting I have heard him say it many times before.

"Lina was my *importante* friend," I say to him. "I love her. You and she are my heroes and I hope that Maria and I will be like the two of you when we are older."

"I know that," he says.

And he does know it, and I know it and the thing is, his solution makes so much sense. There is an ancient order, an ancient rhythm to it and you can call me a fool, but when you look out across the Castropignano expanse of the valley up by the *Castillo* and see through the grainy atmosphere of a twilight sky, the orange flames rolling slowly in the distance across a textured fieldscape, you just understand it all at once. *Capisce. Divino.*

For me, it depends how you like to see it, it takes two to grow. It takes two to make this life. Even memories are a spirit, an entity, a companion. It is okay. You have to fix things for someone. There is no point to a garden if you just grow it for yourself. The wine is for you and for me. Your flowers are my flowers. A cherry tree will not grow if there is not another cherry tree near it. But you do it the way you like to do it, and I will too.

"There is no way I would do somebody else's laundry," Mary says in the early days of suffering that only daughters can know.

"I know," I say, still wondering about the whole thing. "These are ancient ways in a modern life."

And for a time, on Rita there is new growth. *Garibaldi* takes all of the ladies to bingo at Weston and Sheppard. There are new, strange dishes appearing in the fridge and it looks fuller. A zucchini is on the counter again. There is more garbage to take out. He is playing cards two doors up. Widowed *nonnas* bring him toys to fix for their grandchildren, lamps in need of new cords and appliances that are broken. He gets calls to install things. Still, she will not live with him but she does take a little money to prepare his meals across the road and shop for the things he will eat. You can tell he is living but he is not making a life.

Garibaldi is still inspecting the problem. The thing is not yet fixed. I have seen him weave an entire basket with branches and then take it apart at the finale because something was wrong, four rows down. I have seen him spend a week, weaving green, white and red (*the green is the basil, the white is the cheese and the red is the sauce*) wire around a glass bowl, working for days to finish off the lip properly. Why anyone would want to weave electrical wire around a glass bowl is beyond me. I fully understand constructing *scopa* and *briscola* card holders, with working lids, out of cereal boxes, but wire on glass?

"Geez, are you still working on that?" I ask.

"It is not right yet," he laughs and shakes his hand in little circles.

Mary tells me one evening that he has placed an ad in *Corriere Canadese* "fiercely Canadian, proudly Italian."

"You're kidding, I say.

Vedovo di 76 anni. Cerca compagnia Zona Jane e Sheppard. Chiamere etc…

"Do you know how many buzzards he is going to get with that ad?" I say in disbelief.

"No, how many?" Mary says facetiously.

He gets a bird of prey and a songbird. There were a few others but they fly off. The first caller is an Italian woman named Pastora. She is down in Toronto somewhere.

"It is almost like the name she had," he says to me, stretching it into a good omen.

Pastora telephones and then comes over for a coffee. She says that the banks will not loan her money. She needs ten thousand dollars. Yes she will cook for him and clean for him and do his laundry but … if he will only help her with her debt. He is smarter than he looks, thinks that ten thousand is quite a lot and eventually gives her three thousand. He makes her sign a little piece of paper that she will pay him back. She signs it because she is honourable. She is a good Italian woman who does what she says. She is dead to me. She soils the nest of her people. At first we plot how to exact three thousand dollars in retaliation but you never know how deep the rot is in her soul and in her family. *Menge.*

The second caller is ready to have a new boarder. A nice man stayed with her for five years but he died. It is hard for her to live alone. Her name is Luisa. She has a life but living alone in the house is—how do you say it?—crushing her. They talk on the phone for an hour each day. Later she will come over for a coffee. He does not want to leave his house. She does not want to leave hers. There is too much at stake. It is like that with Italian couples when they are married. She loves him. He loves her. Together, the house flourishes. When she dies, he dies, the house dies. To leave the house is to accept death. You have to be ready—there is no rush—to accept death.

By now *Garibaldi* has built a little memorial to his wife. Fittingly, it is in the downstairs kitchen. Typically, he has constructed the corner shelf unit with its four tiers out of old bedposts and spare, triangular pieces of wood that he cut in the garage. On it he hangs her picture, *onetwo* of his poems, a few treasured things and pictures of his son, his daughter, his four grandchildren. He is no longer at the head of the table and sits where she sat so he can get a full view of the work he created with his two hands. Before Christmas he gets a six-foot piece of plywood, paints it white and drills holes in it, to place tiny lights to spell the words: *alla memoria della mia consorte.* He proudly and deliberately hangs this on the balcony for everyone to know. *Buon Natale.*

"Well," Luisa says finally when he persists that he does not want to leave his house, "if you see it differently, you call me."

Scene 3.

A Songbird

A songbird lands on an albicocco *branch.* Il Vagabondo
and his people row Garibaldi *to the new world.*

One evening *Garibaldi* calls us to announce that he intends to
move over to Luisa's house.

"It is for the best. It is what I want to do," he tells us, sounding
sort of distant, removed, like someone who knows us but is not that
close.

"Are you sure this is what you want? Do you trust her?" I ask him
later.

"Yes," he says. His mind is resolute.

"It is time that you meet her," he tells Mary over the telephone.
"We are having supper on Tuesday and I want you to come. My sister
is coming down and I will call your brother. You can see what the
situation is like. We will talk."

Maria is the daughter of her mother. She has vested authority. It
is so subtle, but she represents the ancient kingdom of Italian women.
You must be enchanted to know about this kingdom, but it is real. I
have seen it. Slowly, gradually, by the proxy of death, she is becoming
the new, young matriarch of the family. The rightful heir to her
mother's throne.

I turn right off Jane onto Rita. Thankfully, it is not Sunday and
there is room at the curb to park. I see by the cars in the driveway that
his sister, his son and his daughter are already present at our curious
summit. I try the door and it is locked. I am slightly irked. It is because

the old guy has got me thinking too much about omens. I ring the bell and Carmine lets me in. Shoes go off, slippers go on and I slide my way to the downstairs kitchen like a skater on thin *ceramica*. I catch Luisa's face in profile as I glance into the kitchen. I don't know if I like her. I don't know if I don't like her. It is hard to know. She is dressed like it is church. She has a stern formal look and her eyes are a little hard.

"*Buongiorno!*" I call out, getting the time of day wrong.

"*Ahh, Ciao*, Hi hon', here is *Il Vagabondo, Buonasera,*" is the happy chorus I hear calling back. There are kisses: two for Enedina, one for *mia amore*, two for Luisa, a slap on the arm for *Garibaldi*, and an urban handshake for Carmine. Salutations complete, I round full circle to the other head of the table coincidentally arriving in front of my Mio glass.

"I will get the wine," I say definitively.

I return to the kitchen and focus now on the distinct aroma of *pesce*, of—how do you call it?—the fish. Enedina and Maria are serving now, as part of the ancient rhythm. *Baccala* in red sauce with *spaghettini*—*Ahh, Dio!*, where are my manners?—the strange and glorious world of pasta is a whole other *lezione*. How could I forget it?

I must tell you again, because that is the way to learn, when I first met Maria and we were courting, one day it was time for lunch. I did not have much. I was a student and I cared little for food, nor was it a priority in my budget. I go to the cupboard and thankfully, cleverly, I have a can of Heinz spaghetti. I will make her my specialty, I say. Place a pot on the stove. Open a can of spaghetti and put it in the pot. Heat till bubbling. Place two pieces of white sliced bread in the toaster. Spread with margarine and top with the spaghetti mixture. Serve with milk.

"I am not eating that," Maria says to me definitively.

"Why not? I thought you liked spaghetti," I say, genuinely surprised.

"That is not food and I am not going out with you ever again. I am leaving. Goodbye!" She says, slamming the door with a definitive Mediterranean gesture.

I am flabbergasted, speechless. I must call her this evening.

"Yes, I will see you again," she says.

"It was either that or beans-on-toast," I say contritely *(shrug shoulders here)*.

The enchanted world of pasta, the soul of *gusto*, it is a metaphor for resurrection. It is—how do you say it?—what heaven, what *paradiso* will be like for you when you die. Trust me on this. The noodles, they start off so fragile, so dry and so lifeless, in full *rigor mortis*. They are laid out flat, curled or twisted, or like shells or stars, ribbed cylinders or smooth. They are sold in nests, or packages with numbers. No. 86, No. 88. *La donna e mobile.* Will you buy *De Cecco*, or *Delverde*? *Loretto e Barilla*? Try them all and then decide who you will sing with. For me, I sing with *De Cecco* or *Delverde* when it is on sale at Garden Foods. Put on Verdi's *Rigoletto* and *ripete*, repeat after me. Put your heart into it like you are yanked up on stage unwittingly, like a tourist in the *Caffe Concerto* to sing with Paolo Foti, Maria Paola Turchetta and Pietro Jang at the Tanagra Ristorante in Rome. Are you ready? *Fettuccine A Nido, No 81.* tap, tap, tap: *Penne Rigate! Penne Rigate. Ditali Tubetti Gemelli Stelline Puntalette Quadratini Filini Anellini Gobbetti. Tacconelli, Orecchini Capelli D'angelo. Bravo, bravo, maestro!*

"*Prego, prego.*"

Like songs, this one takes four minutes. That one takes nine minutes. This one takes twelve minutes. Always make too much. Add salt. Watch the pieces softly resurrect and fly in circles. Like Dante, it is truly *magnifico*.

And on earth, Enedina serves baked whitefish while Maria follows with an enchanted pasta and … beans. There are two kinds of olives, a basket of bread and enough of everything for three helpings. Have some more: for me. There is the sponge cake with *biscotti* and fruit for dessert.

"You look more Italian than she does," Luisa remarks and we all laugh. Maria has light blonde hair and a matrimonial surname that could curiously make her staunchly Irish.

"It is because of him," I say pointing to *Garibaldi*, "and his *vino* and his food. They have—how do I say it in your language?—they have enchanted me. I am like the Canadian flyer shot down in occupied Italy, befriended by an entire hill town of Italians and hidden from the Germans. The war is over and I decide to stay. Maria is my war bride!" I say triumphantly, trying not to look like *Il Duce*. (*I never get tired of that story, don't you see? It is why I tell it to you twice.*)

Carmine is laughing his happy laugh.

"Ahh, I see," Luisa smiles. The sternness disappears from her eyes.

We say the Italian prayer, led by Angelo, and they all cross themselves, Catholic-style.

Later, I will ask Mary if Luisa asked if she was *Catolica?*

"No," she says. "She was asking if you were Catholic."

"Oh," I say.

Suddenly, we are talking seriously, authentically and with emotion. It feels very ancient. Enedina is sitting over here. Mary is sitting where Lina would. Carmine is on this side, next to Luisa. Angelo is at that head of the table. I am opposite him. They are going to make some sort of life and we are interviewing them about it. We are ancient chaperones and they are asking our opinion, answering all questions, weathering all scrutiny. I know that what is going to happen has already come to pass, that they are not children and that today is a respectful courtesy. The ghost of Donato Macoretta is in the room with us and then I make him go.

We talk about widowhood, the suffocation of loneliness, there are some tears and then the conversation shifts to business.

"It is not a lot when you add things up. I will cook for him and buy groceries, I will clean his clothes. I will sew his buttons on when he misses one. In return, he will have a companion. I will go places with him, like to bingo, if he asks. Believe me, my dears, I can get along by myself and have plenty to do, but I will go with him if he wants. There is a garden in the backyard and tools he can use," she concludes.

We talk about power of attorney, the old tenant who just died, *Garibaldi's* four grandchildren and Luisa's children who are conducting a similar ancient interview.

"I do not want to disrespect either of you," I say. "We love Angelo and we want what is best for him. How do you know that this is right and that it will work out?"

"We know," *Garibaldi* says, convincingly.

"Our generation is different," Luisa offers. "At our age, we know these things. We want the same things. I am afraid to live alone in the house at nights. Loneliness will kill you slowly."

"I can't believe, in this day and age, he is going to get what he actually wants," I say later on, to Mary. Wisdom is sometimes forged from sadness. Her eyes are black and swept back to her mother in the ancient kingdom. It is raining there now, but she knows it will clear. She will make it clear. It is called suffering and you get courage from it.

Because I am *Il Vagabondo*, I ride her coattails to the ancient place.

"They are both wise *innocenti*," I say to her drying my eyes and talking the lovely dialect of the Court. "They know what they are getting into and they are basically allowing us to get over it and interview them to see what goes. It is respectful," I conclude, shrugging my shoulder, head slightly to the left.

"I know. But I just really miss Mamma."

"Yes," I say. "She loves you and he still loves *her*."

Maybe in the old days when you are poor, when you have nothing, all you have is each other. You have relationships. All the stories about working hard all day, the women coming to bring food, sleeping over under the stars in corn huts constructed in fields, coming back home dead-tired, to shuck and pile corn and then sing and dance and escape the gaze of the old to be with the young—this is why loneliness kills my Italians. It is almost a primeval comfort of presence they are speaking of, deeper than anything I can ever know in this disposable society of disorder and runaway adults. They are like our cat, Peach-of-the-Serengeti, or one of Enedina's unnamed garden felines; they need to be around each other. They are restoring a life and it does grow like grain or like a corn plant in a fallow field the year after the harvest. He will fix things, she will cook. They will take meals together. They will go on outings. She has her own place in the house, he will have his. She is landlord, he is tenant. Together they will restore the enchantment to the garden and the enchantment to the kitchen. Life has a use for Italian women and for Italian men and you need both the heart and the lungs if you are going to sing. *Volare!* It depends how you like to do it though. Everyone does it their way but set down your troubles; settle your piece of land and come home.

"Now we will go over to my house and have a little *espresso* and you can look around," Luisa offers. We disband.

The name of the street keeps nagging at me so I look it up. El Dorado. Did you know that the Incas called it "*Paititi*" which coincidentally sounds vaguely Italian? Everything does to me now. The fabled city of gold, the mystical place that the Spaniards were convinced was the last refuge of the Incas when they fled with all of their treasures. If I told you that one of the streets on the way over, after you say farewell to Rita, is named Courage, that you have to traverse the Spenvalley and pass by the curiously named Ladyshot, I know that you will think that I am a *pagliaccio,* or perhaps you will say that someone has hit me with the *malocchio*, the Evil Eye, and you will no longer believe in the living opera or in my Tales of *Gusto* and Enchantment. I tell you it is all true.

You can tell the street over there is a little richer than my beautiful Rita. The houses are a little larger, much like *Woodibridgi* and nobody comes out that much, at least as far as I can see. The properties are kept beautifully, though, and the trees are pruned to a T, literally, or a stolid Y, cut in the same bold Italian pruning font.

"I don't think I am going to get to know this street that well," I say to Mary and I wonder to myself if it is prophecy, grief or fable that speaks. But the house? I know I am going to get along with it. The driveway is clean. There are flowers out front. There is a side yard and you can see the yard barn from it. The garden is bigger than *Garibaldi's* and there are fruit trees and a patio table on some clean cement slabs. I see plastic chickens and lions, migrated from arid Rita, bringing along their bright red geraniums with them and the ever present black and blue fifty-gallon drums. Purple *vin bon* pails hop around like rabbits and when my eyes focus, there are little systems everywhere.

I have already introduced you to the *cantina* inside, but I do not really want to talk about this house anymore. There is another house that we must say good-bye to first.

Due Intervallo

Il Vagabondo and his people butcher an Italian house

Il Vagabondo addresses his audience:
Ahh, you are stretching your legs, good. Before you go out for a glass of wine and some conversione, stay for a moment and I will share an ancient art with you.

"When it is time to slaughter the pig, we waste nothing," *Garibaldi* tells me one day. He is already back in Castropignano and I can tell he wants me to catch up. "You buy it when it is little, you give it some food and you raise him up to be big. We had maybe *onetwo* pigs at a time. That was all we had the money for. When the pig was big it was time to kill it. My grandfather knew the way. He knew how to do it. You hoisted it up over the branch of a tree and you cut his neck so he would bleed. We even collected the blood and made it like a sausage," he says cutting up an invisible casing and placing the pieces in the cooking pan I rescued.

"It is a good house," the Vietnamese fellow next door says to me twice, like he is hoisting something on a rope.

He notices the For Sale sign on the front lawn.

"Your father is moving?" he asks.

"He is my father-in-law, and yes he is moving," I say. "He does not want to be alone."

I want to be alone, to look at the house a little bit, but the neighbour persists. I can see he is assessing with a measured stare into the garage, up over the steps by the *cantina*, through the branches of the peach tree and down the side yard to the back. I am vaguely irked and say good-bye to him, turning to busy myself with nothing in the garage. When he goes away, I come back out to look at the For Sale sign again. It is in a metal frame designed for its purpose.

"Typical," I sneer to myself. For a minute I think of all the elections, the municipal, the provincial, the federal, and I laugh at the image of hundreds of signs staked into the front lawn. They represent all political parties and *Garibaldi* and his friends in North York support everyone equally until it is time to vote. They are flags of convenience to the Italian gardener so long as the stakes are made of good, clean wood. It is a small secret I share. Everything has a purpose. Everything can be recycled. *Capisce?*

But this one metal sign, buffeted by a shivering February wind, is a magnet. Within a day and a half, the house is on the market, sold, possession in July. A clean, quick stroke. It is deep. The house bleeds out. It is dead. Like the pig, we must cut him up, let nothing go to waste.

So we do. It is already a Spartan environment. (It is the people not the furniture that make a home.) First, we cut out a bed, the crucifix, a filing cabinet, the dining room table, the hutch, my precious Mio glass, some furniture and other entrails. I rent a truck and my son Nico and I haul it all over to golden El Dorado. Decisively and with sharp, clean strokes, Carmine gets his portion of the inside, Mary gets hers. We leave some leftovers for the new owners and the guts are taken over to the church. Alone in cupboards remain a few pots and plates in the kitchen, for we will have our last supper when the work is done.

We cut to the outside. We are in the garage now. The automatic door shuffles stupidly up and stops with a jerk. The useful things are separated and divided into three portions. A good carcass is left. There is still some meat on bones that can be boiled down and used: a spare ladder, countless jars and oily wooden boxes of bolts, irregular pieces of plank, of plywood, of lumber—the good Italian spine of it.

But curiously, it is the outside that we dress with a most tender care and with the sharpest of blades. It is the choice section. Everything represents her. The forsythia is gently pried out with the shovel, so tenderly we remove root from soil. We rap the holy bulb with burlap, moisten it and slip green plastic garbage bags over the entire muddy thing before hoisting it onto the truck. It will be placed in our side yard. Another shrub, I don't know how you call it in the language of your choice, is tenderly separated from its cement border. Next year purple flowers will burst forth in Bolton. Every rose bush is cut out and lifted, divided into portions and hauled away. Next, the tiny organs are removed; the silver dollar plants, the yellow flowers and the pink ones. I take the rest of the purple pails and stack them in my yard barn. It is like I am removing the feet of the pig. We take our breaks to sit in the sun on lawn chairs even though it is cool.

Spring comes, then June, and I stand by the grapevine, next to the metal shed. I see the little *kiki* begin to develop anew. The grapes are green and hard, not yet plump. I run my hand along the hairy central vine, up and over my head to where the old reliable bark gives way to slender new branches green and tender. I rub the tiny leaves and trail their serrated edges with my index finger. I am talking to them softly, in the grower's dialect. My eyes catch a white malevolent cluster of hard, hidden half-grown berries. Cancerous non-grapes with black spots on the bottom. They shriek at me. I pinch the stem off with my thumbnail and crush it underfoot, violently, like a Castro-pignano scorpion.

It is time—there is no rush—for a last supper. I am well versed now in the art of making sauce. I know how to ladle the thick red mixture so gently, so lovingly in rings over plates of steaming pasta. It is my gift. But it is the smell—I want it to pervade the entire downstairs one last time, swirling within the kitchen, wafting around the corner to the furnace room and the back *cantina*, lifted on wings up the ceramic stairs to tempt the ceremonial rooms that we spend so little time in; continuing the sensual flow across the little downstairs room where we watch television and finally, out to the entrance to mix with the age-old musty smell of the primary *cantina*. Like a bouquet of flowers, it is here that I look underneath the clean wooden planks, softly stained purple from the wine and etch "I love *Nonna*," then I seal the door to that sacred tomb for the last time.

"She probably even cleans under here!" I sad-laugh to myself and pat her imaginary hair-do ever so lightly.

For dessert, we stand and weep by the cherry tree in full bloom. I spit the bones out at the children. They are startled that a grown up would dare enter into their realm. Within a shocked second they spit bones back, scoring direct hits, laughing. We rub our hands along the smooth bark and feel the knots. The tree is too big to butcher. I would cut that out too but this must be the new owner's portion. His share of the meat. His share of the fertility and of the prosperity. We ask the children to go up into the tree, to relive an older happier time. We take their picture and re-enact when their *nonna* let them climb and pick and climb and pick and climb and pick forever while barbecue smoke and planes fly over. The *nipote* understand that it is a good-bye act in the grand *opera*. I am pleased.

I wipe my tired brow. The job is done. Nothing is wasted. Everyone now has their share.

I have kept you too long. Go and have some wine. You are working too hard. You deserve it. It is for you and for me. Pass a little time, and I will flash the lights when it is time to ritorno, ciao.

(Gently, the lights are turned off and then on, off and then on.)

Perfetto. Come with me now! It is time to go forward to El Dorado. It exists! There are treasures to be found, more tales of gusto and enchantment, and new lezione to be learned. I will show you how to make the sauce and then, you can go home.

Act VI

[Act VI]

Scene 1.

The Life in El Dorado.

Garibaldi *is on the far bank*. Il Vagabondo *hitches the ferry
and decides to stay and stir the* polenta.

If you intend to stop and get a bread at Molisana at Jane and Highway
7 you must go early. Trust me on this. If you can't get a bread,
don't worry. You won't leave empty-handed. Get something else. The
bruschetta is so light. The way the oil soaks into the crust is beautiful.
You are a *buffone* if you only buy one slice. The pizza is good, you
should try it. You can get the buns on Eddystone at Commisso or,
like I say, La Stella is your second choice. It is however, the first choice
for strange and unusally shaped cookies with almonds in them. I forget
how you call it, but they somehow melt when you snap one in your
mouth. You better go quick because it is different now. Ferlisi's has
been taken over by a wholesale store. Valencia emigrated to parts unknown. She moves aside for Sieu Thi Vinh Phong-Yong Feng Super-
market Inc. You must try the Uncle Chen's "*Chiliciously*" hot chilli
garlic sauce in aisle 2A on your potatoes. Or perhaps on your *risotto*,
try the Saigon Hot Sauce packed by Vena Hung. They are both
exquisite. Lamentably, Yong Feng does not stock Rastrelli oil.

The telephone rings and I remember an old joke.

One of the best ways to tease your Italian hosts— these are the
elders I am talking about—is to bring them tomatoes in August. It is
guaranteed to create a happy argument.

"*Ehh?* Why do you bring these? We have so many in the garden
already. The *cantina* is full. What will we do with them now?"

"*Senora*, you are making me—how do I say it?—nervous. I thought you liked tomatoes. *(Make an Il Duce face here and shrug)* It is wrong for you to return my gift. How can you do this?"

I must tell you that I know from the experience, if you bring them a zucchini, they will see through you immediately and the women will give you a smack. You may wish to experiment with the thing, but … you have been warned.

"Maria, *come sta*?" Luisa says.

"*Bene, senora, grazie.*"

"How are the children? Are they okay? We are back now. You must come for lunch. Enedina will be there and she is bringing her friend Nunziata. We will look at the pictures of the Hometown. There is nothing to bring, we have everything," Luisa says to my wife.

Il Vagabondo is always glad to go. You never know what you will find and the company is so good. There are Tales of *Gusto* and Enchantment in every visit, no matter how short or how long.

Yes, I could tell you more about the trip across the river to El Dorado with *Garibaldi* but I don't know if it is that important and besides there is a little compost in it for me and my people. I do not wish to move it. There are other lessons to learn.

"When we first came here it was in the win-ter!" *Garibaldi* says to me, one day at the new table, cracking the syllables of his last word into two. I feel the pieces clatter and slip across his memory in bits.

"We took the train from New York up to Toronto and from there we got to Montrose. We lived in the same house with two other families. I think after that first year if we had the money to go back we would go back. It was so hard. But we had the debt to pay and there was nothing to go back to. After the war, the land was ruined. There was nothing," he repeats wistfully.

Somehow, I feel the same way, but for totally different reasons.

"I was worried when you went back home, you would see the life they had there and that then you would regret that you even came to Canada," I say to him seriously. "When I saw the view from the *Castillo*, I didn't want to come home. It was scary."

"I am glad to be back," he says thoughtfully, "and it was good to go."

I listen and wait.

The Court of *Garibaldi* is a winepress and the Tales of *Gusto* and Enchantment are the juice. The old guys know what I am talking about. There is nothing more satisfying. The press is full with clusters of purple Carignane grapes. They are authentic and taste better if you drop them on the garage floor. Your hands are vaguely cold. Pick up the stained half-moon blocks and fit them perfectly on top of clusters around the threaded pole. There is hardly any space between their outer edge and the smooth, stained inside of the slats. Fit the next two rectangular blocks snugly against the threads and perpendicular to the crack where the crescents join. Place the cam and turning assembly over the stem, start it and then spin it smoothly through the palms of your hands, until it rests tightly upon the blocks. Now comes the best part. Place a clean orange pail under the smooth black spout of the cast-iron base. Pick up the black steel bar and fit it into the hole on the turning assembly. When you are ready—there is no rush—give it *twothree* good, solid pulls, feel the muscles respond along your forearm and shoulders and watch the satisfying turn of the cog grip down, held in place by the little steel locking lever. It is exactly here that all time and space stops. There is nothing to think about. There is nothing to worry about. There is only the creative tension of hard work and love. Cause and effect delay until the magic moment when, suddenly, juice swells out around the base, pulsing to begin its thin ripe stream into the orange pail. It is everything.

But what I tell you now will be lost soon. It has to be that way. Yes, somebody was smart enough to ship over a couple of huge *centrali*, the giant wooden casks that stood proudly at the mouth of the little nursery at Islington and Steeles, northwest side. I enjoyed them for a while, but they are gone. Nobody crushes grapes anymore with their feet. You don't need to over here, it's okay.

Yes, you can buy your juice or your wine in twenty-litre pails and you will never need the machine. Stained wooden slats are not being replaced, cast iron bases are rusting, good solid steel turning bars are misplaced. The last time we went, we put cardboard against the back seat of the van. For every five, you get an extra pail. We got ten Grenache, a cabernet sauvignon and a Portofino red. *Garibaldi* is pleased that we are experimenting with juice of higher quality.

"See? You should stick with me," I tell him. "You old guys think you know, but you don't know.

Finally, they load the heavy pails into your truck, wrapped in green garbage bags to catch the excess juice on the lids. I don't know how they do it where you are, but when you get the pails they put a little puncture hole in the lid to allow for expansion in case the juice starts to ferment in the sealed pail. I am sure the wives made them improve on the process.

"*Mamma Mia*, why do they do it like this? Every year you come home and the van is a mess. There is a better way. Don't be such a *testa dura*, tell them…"

We approach El Dorado from Driftwood to Spenvalley now, make a right. You can bypass Rita altogether that way. Sometimes I will go by there when I am *Il Vagabondo* and it is not a Sunday but most times, I go straight.

The doorbell rings. We come in. There are kisses and hugs. We are welcome in this home. Enedina's eyes look upon her niece lovingly. Nunziata is blessed with a face that smiles happily in repose.

"This is *Il Vagabondo*. He is not Italian. He is better than an Italian boy," is the way I am introduced by my friend, Luisa. There is laughter. I look sidelong. If *Garibaldi* is happy then I am happy. It is a gift. She is one of my Italians, now.

"Ah, I see," I say. "You say that because I bring your plates and your empty Tupperware containers back."

"You are right," says Luisa.

"*Ciao, Garibaldi*," I say. "I have two empty bottles for you now and I am not sure what to do with them or where to put them. Do you think I should take them to the *cantina*?"

"No," he says simply.

The children disappear to drink orange pop. The women begin their happy catching up talk and because I am smarter than I look, I join Luisa at the stove.

"Here. Take this and stir," she commands, passing over the stem of a very large wooden spoon, stuck in a beautiful yellow mixture.

Stirring *polenta* has nothing to do with the delicate turns of oil and vinegar. It is hard work and you have to keep your eyes on it. It is an enchanted food, however, because when it is ready, it is ready. Do not serve it if your guests are not reliable and are not already in your home. Here is what you do. Get a large pot and fill it half full with water. Heat it until just before it is going to boil; let it ride the edge of the tipping point. Add butter and salt. You may add the *polenta* now in slow, loving circles that spin up memories. Some may use the fine corn flour, but me, I prefer the coarse grain. Begin to stir now to infinity. Keep adding the corn flour and make sure you do not let it boil. If you are doing it right, you will begin to get a beautiful yellow texture, not as consistent as *Inglese* mashed potatoes, more moist-like. I forgot to tell you, in another large pot you are simmering some homemade tomato sauce. Don't be nervous, soon I will show you how to make it. The *polenta* is magically beginning to take form. It becomes thicker. Begin to turn down the heat now and have your trusted assistant call all guests to the table. If you are playing *la musica*, now is a good time to put it on. Your assistant will put out the large flat bowl of steaming pork shoulder and beside it, a slightly smaller, wide bowl of raggedy homemade sausage and *grande* meatballs. You have already thawed your Caravaggio mudcat and prepared the thin red strips in a small, white dish of oil, garlic, basil and *prezzemolo*. (*"Ehh, I am not going to translate the last word for you. You should know this by now."*) Put it on the table beside four different kinds of bread in a basket, some sweet chard from Nunziata's garden, mixed green salad with homemade dressing and the inevitable little wooden bowl of roasted almonds. You have already made room for the orange pop, the *aqua*, the Mio, the wine and *onetwo* bottles of *benezene* (*birra*, gas).

Afterwards, I will set before you a large bowl of *la frutta*; the kiwi, the orange, the apples and the grapes. *Espresso* will be on and I have prepared for you one of Enedina's sponge cakes, (*it is like a bird, it is so light*); a homemade apple pie with a nice, tender crust and always too many of the hard, icing like cookies that melt in your mouth.

"Did your mothers teach you how to make all of these desserts when you were little?" I make the happy mistake of asking the three feminine elders at the table.

"*Mamma mia, no!*" they all laugh in exasperated chorus.

"We learned how to make it when we came here, when we were married," they all say.

"You see, back then, we could not afford much, the sugar and the special flour and the the—how do you call it?—the ingredients you need to make these things. We did not have the oven, like we do now. We just had a fire and some flat stones to cook on. Maybe at Christmas, yes, we would trade a rabbit for some sugar or some eggs. Then we would take them to the town, to the baker to have them made. If we had a hen, we used the eggs to barter for things. Like, the cobbler to fix your shoes."

"How many eggs would it take to fix your shoes?" I ask, intrigued by the barter system.

"Maybe about *twelvethirteen*," Enedina instructs.

A thousand questions are cracked open and whisked into shape in my mind.

Mamma Mia! I have forgotten the polenta!

It is a perfect texture now. Turn off the heat. Clean off the long wooden stirring spoon. With a ladle, place a good portion on a plate and flatten it out with the rounded underside, like a … like a pancake. *Perfetto.* Now with the same underside, make a little trough around the circumference. This will catch the sauce and keep it all on top of the *polenta.* It is *importante* to know this. You do not want to waste the sauce. Now ladle the thick red mixture with a languid spin on top of the yellow wheel. Dust liberally with *parmesan* and *romano* cheese and watch it melt into beautiful shapes. The children will say reading the cheese is like reading the clouds. There are pictures in it. It is part of the enchantment. Repeat the process for as many guests as you have at the table and have your assistant serve. Quickly sit down, *Garibaldi* will say the Italian prayer, *Chin Chin* and you are having lunch in the Court.

"Angelo," I say. How did you like it in Italy, in your Hometown, was it better?"

"Not really," he says unexpectedly like a bubble popping on sauce and I know there is a thick storied sea underneath.

"Yes," he begins, "I liked to see my sister and my brother and their families. It has been forty-eight years and Biagio was so amazed that I remembered where everything was and the names of all of the people." ("Biagio is my friend," I interject.) "It was like all my memories;

they flooded back to me at once. We went everywhere and saw everyone and I like that. We went to the cemetery with Nicola and I saw
my parents' grave but ..." he says with characteristic emphasis and I
know that his index finger is signalling a lesson, "... it is not there
now like it used to be."

"How so?" I say, taking the bait.

"It is the food," he says. "They grow it but they do not use it. It
all goes to waste now. When we arrived, the figs were ready. Nicola
took us to my wife's house and they were falling off the trees. We had
so many figs to eat. And the wild vine was filled with beautiful clusters
of yellow grapes. Not like you can get over here. Better. Luisa was
picking them and we wanted to bring them all back with us. But they
just go to waste there. Nobody wants them. It was not like that when
I left. You were lucky if there was any fruit left on the tree or the vine
when they were ready."

"Did you get stung?" I ask, teasing him.

"No," he says ignoring me.

"We walked in their gardens and they stepped on the big cabbages.
We put some in bags but there were too many. It is like they have
more time and they are still growing things but there is too much
food now, nobody wants it. It is not right."

I understand now why it is good to go and good to be back.

The conversation shifts.

"Have some more *espresso*," Luisa tells me.

I defer to everyone else.

"No, you have it," Luisa persists.

I accept. My little cup is refilled to the brim and the pot is finished.
What can I say? (*shrug shoulders here*) Il Vagabondo is an honoured
member of *la famiglia*.

"Good," declares Luisa in her strong voice. "Now I can prepare a
fresh pot for the others!"

There is laughter.

Later, the women clear the table and I make a point of helping to
purposely disturb the ancient order. It is my *Inglese* butterfly effect. I
don't mind. *Garibaldi* and I are left at the table. I am across from him.
We sit with isosceles elbows, fingers clasped, our mouths resting on
them with our thumbs under our chin. It is the spontaneous prayer

of the content, the time when old men will listen to young men. I have seen it.

For some reason the wine press doesn't matter as much anymore. Yes, it is a beautiful machine: a sacred Michelangelo—the cast-iron statue of the garage winery, an *importante* thing of life but not the life itself. What we did with the *libretto* and who we were with, that is the thing!

"Angelo," I say quietly, "it was good to go with you to see where you get the wine, to see how it is done. Now I will know how to do it when you can't go."

"Yes," he says simply.

Scene 2.

Venus de *Gnocchi*

If it is giovedi, *it must be time again for* la scuola

A quick stop at Commisso's on Eddystone and they still do not have their Renaissance Paintings calendar for the New Year. Consequently, *Il Vagabondo* arrives empty-handed on the clean El Dorado driveway at ten after the *bella sette* in the morning.

"*Il Vagabondo* is on time," I say, rapping the glass door to the kitchen with my knuckles, sliding it back and entering triumphantly.

"It is not true. You are ten minutes late!" Luisa greets me with a smile. *Garibaldi* looks up from his Italian crossword, focuses and then returns to his paper. Three across: seven letter word for joker.

"Ahh ... so you say," I shrug. "It is hard for me to believe." There are kisses.

I am at the table now. We discuss our personal health, the health of our children and the health of my wife. We conclude that we get old and we get sore and before I know it, I am downstairs in the basement kitchen ready for *Gnocchi* School. I am given a pair of slippers to put on. It is a good sign. Our work table is right beside the furnace and it is dominated by a large flat, clean sheet of warm wood. Behind us: the sink, the air conditioning *sistemi* with its valves and its hoses; the gas burners, pots and pans, ladle after ladle suspended happily beside the beautiful spice rack riveted sturdily into the tin exhaust hood over the stove. The bare bulb of the basement light sheds a sleepy glow. Beside us, in another area, *Garibaldi* is at a little workbench repairing a drawer so that it will open and shut smoothly.

I hear him singing.

La scuola begins. Luisa instructs me. Place into the pot ten medium sized potatoes with their skins on. Boil them for about twenty minutes or so and then drain the water. Take a small teaspoon and peel off the skins. Put the skins in the pail that will go to the compost. *Bene bene.* Put the potatoes into a ricer and mash them. Complete the process with a different tool to get the texture nice and smooth-like. Dump the mashed potato on your clean board and spread them out so they can cool. Have a banana.

Crack three eggs and whisk them. Spread the potatoes into a donut shape on your board and put the eggs into the centre. Rinse the bowl with a tiny bit of water or, if you like to do it that way, with *poco poco* milk and pour it onto the eggs. *Bene.* Prepare two cups flour. Sprinkle liberally over the potato mixture and pour a third cup into a bowl. Place it next to you to use for occasional sprinkles or for cleaning your hands.

Now you must knead the potatoes, the eggs, the flour together. Learn to say *farina* instead of flour. Add some more *farina* when you need to and soon you will have a nice, beautiful ball of potato dough blended perfectly. (*I can't believe you take such an interest in these things.*) Roll it out a little bit until it is about a foot long then slice it on an angle along the length. Dust your hands with *farina*. See, you are the expert now! Take each slice and roll it along the board, pressing and rolling, pressing and rolling until you have a slender dough-snake about *eighteentwenty* inches long. Let the kids help you with this part.

It is at this exact point that I am reminded of snake stories from earlier meals. It is a fact that I collect these stories. They slither around and coil in my memory and I cannot believe they are all true. *You tell me.*

A husband and wife are sleeping. The husband wakes up and notices a snake sliding down the mouth of the sleeping woman. He does nothing to wake her and sees the tail of the snake go down her throat. She is pregnant. They go to the doctor's and he cannot do anything until the baby is born. The Wife must drink the milk for the snake, every day, to keep her stomach out of turmoil. When it is time for the delivery, the snake, it comes out first!

A mother gives birth to a baby. The baby is so fussy, always crying and not gaining weight. The mother was healthy before but she is not really doing well after the baby is born. People wonder if it is a snake that comes in through the little round hole in the bottom of the door they use to let the cat in. To prove it, they spread ash from the fire onto the floor. The next morning they see the tell-tale path of the snake-glide along the floor. The baby gets better.

A variation on this story: a cow gives birth to a calf. The calf is not—*how do you say it?*— thriving. The people notice some movement in the grass underneath where the mother cow is feeding. They approach the grass, and there affixed to the udder of cow, the snake is drinking. They kill it. The calf gets better.

And did you know, I say to myself, recalling both the memory and the meal, while pressing, smoothing and rolling, pressing, smoothing and rolling the *gnocchi*; in the Hometown they had large, thick snakes. I see Angelo cupping his hands to suggest girth and I am reminded of *Inglese* fish stories of the ones that got away. But he is sincere and the elders are all nodding. The heads of these snakes are huge, like a cat's head with the ears pointing back. Enedina last saw one when she was there in '86. She is serious.

I am gently pulled free from these memories by the melody in the room next door.

"Angelo," I call out teasingly, "can you sing: 'Over the Hill and Far Away?'" It is an old joke of my father's.

"Not really," he says, ignoring me.

Later I will tell Mary that *Garibaldi* barely came into the room to speak with me.

"It was like I was invisible," I complain. "I liked the work but there were no stories, no conversations. All he did was come in and ask Luisa if she showed me how to flip the *gnocchi* with the tines of a fork," I scowl.

"He never helped Mamma when she made *gnocchi*," she instructs. "That was her job, not his," she reminds me, illustrating a lesson of the ancient order.

"There are some things I don't … I don't agree with," I say mocking the dialect of the Court.

"Good," she says.

***

This is the time to start a big pot of water boiling on the large burner. On the little burner you have some red sauce simmering. Take some cooked *rapini* from the freezer and let it thaw over very low heat in a shallow pan with a lid. Definitely add oil and garlic. On the other large burner, it is good that you have some pork shoulder simmering in its own juices. Just before we are ready to serve, I want you to prepare a cup of homemade red vino, turn up the heat and pour the red liquid onto the meat … watch and smell the steam. *Perfetto*.

Turn around now, to the table. Take a knife and cut your remaining *gnocchi* into little angled shapes about an inch long. Take the tip of your index finger and gently press, slightly below the imaginary halfway line of *gnocchi*. Pull your finger back and the technique is to flip the *gnocchi* over. The dent you left in it holds a tiny pool of sauce when you serve. Do this to all of them. You will be able to serve six robustly with ten potatoes.

Like the pied piper of *gusto*, let all the little *gnocchis* run off and dive into the hot water. Bring to boil, stirring occasionally. After *twelvethirteen minutes,* maybe a little more, use a draining ladle, pull the *gnocchi* out and place in a steel bowl. Put a little sauce in the bottom first. In layers add sauce and dust liberally with cheese; another layer, add sauce, dust with cheese. Cover the bowl and place it back on the top of your pot. It will act as a double boiler and keep your *Venus de Gnocchi* sculpture warm. Good for you.

Let us go upstairs now, to the table.

Garibaldi has decanted some wine. Say the Italian prayer and our conversation turns to making corn brooms. Get the branch of a tree and three heads from a plant that grew like the corn, but was primarily just the silk on the tips. Take three heads, nail the centre one in with a little nail and if you know how to do it, peel the stem from the stalk right down the middle and use the fibrous lengths to bind the heads tightly to your stick. There it is—the corn broom. Now you know how to do it.

It is midafternoon when I say *arrivederci* to drive south on Keele to Maple Leaf. There is another Italian street there that is changing amidst the rising and setting of the sun in *Garibaldi's* Court. Another one of my *paesanos* is grieving. We talk, I leave. His stories weave together in a perfect segue of a hard life lived well. He is taking stock of his journey from Welland, to Niagara, to Toronto, to Italy, and back to Toronto with his family. What is it with us? The women seem to go first all the time. It is too much. As I leave, one of his daughters pulls into the clean driveway. Our windows automatically go down and we laugh and say hello. Silver cars never look dirty. Black ones do.

"You know, you can also put *ricotta* in the *gnocchi* instead of potato," Angie calls out happily. "If you do that you should also get some frozen spinach, thaw it, cut it up really fine and add it to the mixture." She is her mother's daughter. It is an ancient *lezione* from the young, learned easily and shared freely in the wind.

"*Grazie*," I say while backing out.

I head west on Maple Leaf, right on Jane, onto the little spur of Black Creek and edge north to enter the busy Highway 400. Soon, *Il Vagabondo* will be an *eroe* in his Court for he triumphantly brings gifts from afar: the *gnocchi*, the *rapini*, the *porco*, the *pane*, *vino* and Tales of *Gusto* and Enchantment.

"You don't kiss your husband any more?" I say to my wife.

"I thought you said you were bringing lots of *gnocchi*," she says to me in disbelief.

"*Hmm*," I say, shrugging.

Finale
and
Curtain

Finale and Curtain

Il Vagabondo *addresses his audience, gives them something to
take home and reveals the secret words on the inner band
of Maria's wedding ring*

Signore e Signori. Ladies and Gentlemen. We have come to our close.
You see, in our Tales of *Gusto* and Enchantment there are no
dragons to slay, no natural disasters to flee from, so little compost to
move-a. No, our tale is told in the slow ambling gait of life approached,
wire weaved, *mosto* squeezed and peppers skinned. *Abbi pazienza.* A
time to pass time, to remember, to perceive, and to stir the polenta.
In the Court of *Garibaldi, lezione* abound! Gardens will live and
gardens will die while we sing *cantos* of love and of loss. Wasps, intoxicated and with no thought of stinging, sing *Dino Martinelli* between
the *kiki.* Zucchini spread their arms in backyard embrace and grow
wildly into the night. We see the art in day and place and street and
interact with it to create our own composition. We add new *paesani*
to our dance and bring them in while others parade past stumbling.
Streets die and *macchina* become obsolete. Steamer trunks are rescued
from garbage heaps, their ancient order preserved. We pray in far
away cemeteries, are loved by friends and eat figs forever. Houses are
butchered in clean, efficient strokes and we collect the blood to make
the sausage. In kitchens we sit, smack tables with our bare hands and
stir our thoughts in the spin of love. Flames clean away our hillside
stubble and we graft anew. Through Providence we meet, we laugh,

we doubt, we suffer, we cry. We think we know, but we don't know. Our shoulders shrug in acceptance and in accepting we go to God, beyond the barriers of language, the old ways, the ancient order and into the living opera, arms outstretched before you onto the rich stage of *Felicita. Felicita.* There is no rush. *Io sono contento. Grazie. Molto grazie.*

The drama of *la famiglia* is the *prima* drama. It is everything. The wine is for you and for me. And because you are leaving, I must give you something to take home. Like *Il Vagabondo*, return to those you love and you will return always with *gusto* and enchantment. It depends how you like to do it, but this is how I do it. It is the way I have been taught.

First, you must remember your mother-in-law, always, and then take a big deep pot and set it on the stove. Take any oil but Rastrelli and pour it slowly, in rings along the bottom. Peel an onion, slice it gently without cutting it apart. Let the sacred tears and the oil mix on a low heat. Let garlic fall, *onetwo* cloves to join the dance. Small bubbles form in the oil and now you must add the pork ribs to singe and to brown. It is time for the salt, the pepper, the basil, the—how do you call it?—the orégano and my secret *Inglese* weapons, the savoury and the sage. Not too much sage. You are turning the ribs now with a fork or tongs. Beautiful. Now remove them. Put them in a nice bowl etched with luscious grape vines or Italian women pouring water. How is your oil? Add some more and let it heat up. It is time to brown the *veale* and maybe some lamb, it depends how you do it. More savoury, more sage. Do not have a banana. If it is past 10:30, you may have a Mio glass of *vino*, only a little. There is no rush. *Perfetto.*

Now you must take three one-litre mason jars of the sauce I showed you how to make. The kids are so fussy, so do not use the jars with the hot peppers in them. They will be marked with rubber bands around the neck of the jar so you can tell the difference. *Mamma Mia!* One time, I made the sauce with the wrong jars. The rubber bands were too old. They broke. It was—how you call it, in your language?—a tragedy. The kids had hot dogs that day. Enedina puts a carrot in now, some people add sugar or a little anis seed, but for me, I do not like those things. I put what Lina puts. A "*dot*". A dot is non-dialect, non-formal *Italiano*, non-*Il Vagabondo*-speak, non-*Inglese*. I tell you there is slang, even in the ancient order. A dot is a bouillion cube. Put *onetwo* in. *Si, si.* Now, you must spoon in three small, thin cans of *Unico* tomato paste. This will thicken your sauce. The difference between the *Inglese* and the Italian? An *Inglese* will buy three cans at a time, or maybe as many as nine if they are on sale. An Italian will buy the entire case. Have them go into the back to get it. Okay. You are ready. Turn the stove up to high and boil the sacred mixture. Now, you may have a second Mio glass of wine. In thirty minutes or so—there is no rush—turn it down to low. Let it simmer for *twothree* hours. Your house will smell so good. As my *Inglese* friends will say, "It is to die for." Here is what you do, if you want to be merry and provoke the ancient order of *Garibaldi's* Court. (*"Ehh,"* I am *Il Vagabondo, it is my prerogative.*") Take a little brown bottle of Kitchen Bouquet. Remove the yellow cap and pour a good splash of the browning fluid into the sauce. If you let them see you do it, you will hear them screeching as far away as Castropignano! A little *Inglese butterfly effect* never hurt anyone. You are after all, a Canadian.

I don't know why you have to go (*why don't you stay and eat? Mangia, Mangia*), but if you must go, let the sauce cool. I will pour it into two pots and use rubber bands to secure the lids. You must always carry the wine in a bag, in case you get stopped by the *carabinieri*. Make sure the pots lie flat. Do not forget to return them if you ever want to get sauce again.

"Maria, why does he not learn to speak in Italian?"

"He is trying," she will say, loyally.

"*Ti amo amore,*" I whisper, like the ocean in the shell. (*shrug shoulders here*)

Final Curtain Call.
Canto: Take Your Time Going, but Hurry Back

Il Vagabondo *addresses his audience and goes home*

Signore e Signori, *the ladies and the gentlemen.*
It is too much. We must part ways and ritorno *to our own Living* Operas. Piacere.

Before you go I must teach you one last lezione *and then you must take it with you to teach someone else how to do it the way you like to do it. Then you can sing in the dialect of love; the ancient rhythm!* Per favore: Do it ... for me!

Observe. This is the way to make the crown of the Inglese Gusto *and Enchantment. If you have married into an Italian family (or any other family) it will make you a* eroe.

Here is the instruc-zione, *complete with dialect, for the traditional* Inglese *high cholesterol meat loaf of the 1950s and the 1960s. It is the way my mother likes to do it so it is really the only way to do it, but (shrug shoulders here) it depends how you like it.*

I must warn you that this meatloaf is so bene *but it is not that good for you and it weighs about thirty pounds. (*Mamma Mia! *it is so dense it is like a free weight.)*

Like the store bought veale, *it will lose its enchantment if you eat it too much. For this, you make it maybe once every twelve weeks or at the end of each week like we used to do if you are running out of the money. You can use it for the sandwiches for the next four days. If you are a kid and you take a sandwich to* la scuola, *your friends will want to trade you for it. Trust me on this. If you take the thing for lunch, make it with lots of margarine, salt and pepper and either HP sauce or if you are a* buffone, *like my brother, green pickle relish.*

I will show you the way so you can get a picture of the thing in your mind. Then you will know how to do it.

Take a meat loaf casserole dish, the butter and a little piece of wax paper to coat the inside of the dish ever so lightly. Take the sharp knife and cut a little sliver of butter and put it in your mouth. *Perfecto.* Now pour yourself a little rye with ice. There is not time to smoke.

In the big green mixing bowl from the era or maybe the yellow one if you still have it, crack three eggs and whisk. Put some milk in and whisk again. Get a pack of onion *zuppa* mix—*he* is my friend and cousin to Lipton Chicken Noodle *zuppa*—the *inglese pollo zuppa* mix of choice. Pour it into the bowl and stir. Now you add the herbs: lots of savoury and not as much sage but more sage than thyme, marjoram and basil. *Bene.* Now you must chop up the *sedano* (it is okay to look it up), very small. Have a sip of rye—there is no rush—find your can opener to open up a can of mushroom pieces and stems. Dump *him* into the mixture, water and all. It is so moist! Give it a little stir to blend in the herbs. Pour in some bread crumbs, not too much, to help with the binding. You have already thawed your ground pork and beef, making sure neither of these are extra lean or lean. If you do it the way I like to do it, make sure you keep the mushroom can to drain off the sea of grease mid-way through the cooking. If your kids are students of the Meatloaf School, explain to them carefully why it is unhelpful to pour the grease down the sink. Teach them to do an *experimento* and put it in the fridge. It will get hard and white and then you can throw *him* out on the garbage day. *Bene.* Crumble up the ground meat into the mixture and knead it all together with your hands. Ah, *scuzzi*, before you do this, make sure you have another little sip of rye because your hands are going to get greasy. The kids will want to work without a net but do not let them. By now your spouse has made an *up and down gesture with her left hand* and has tied an apron around your waist because inevitably you are wearing your best T-shirt. This is a good time to kiss.

Your meatloaf mixture should be nice and moist now. Take a little ball of it and put it in your mouth. Remember in the 1950s and the1960s there was the bogey man but not the tape worm so it is okay to do it this way. Scare the kids though because the raw meat is so good they will want to eat it too much. So will you. I tell you, if you eat it too much, you will get a—how do we call it?—a snake in you. I have seen it.

By now you have asked someone to turn the stove to 325 because your hands are so greasy. Use the middle oven rack. Bake for an hour and a half, take it out of the oven and let it stand for *couple* minutes. Pour your children some *Goofy Grape* and shoo them away. There is time to finish your rye and have a smoke because after all, back then, even the *dottore* were lighting up and encouraging you to do the same (*shake head here*. This is *Inglese* head-dialect for *I can't believe we actually lived this way.*)

Call your Italians to the table, *Garibaldi*, your mother-in-law, the *nipote*, your beautiful wife. The children will have Mio, pear juice or orange pop. Maria will be happy. The *old guy* will look serious and slightly out of place like he is in an upstairs (translate: never-used) kitchen. Put on your rare recording of *Opera Without Words: The Barber of Seville, Rome Symphony Orchestra* on the German Label: Kapp. Serve with silky mashpotatoes and steamed carrots with process cheese (do not use *cheez whiz*). If you are feeling *dramatico*, sprinkle on a little walnut crumbs. Say the Italian prayer and begin the new Tale of *Gusto* and Enchantment. Make sure you offer your mother-in-law at least three helpings. She of course, will look worried around the eyes, like she is waiting for the bus. She is not comfortable, the chairs are not right; she is not in her own home, but she loves you too much and this is more than enough.

Addio